FACING GOLIATH
A JOURNEY OF HOPE

Copyright © 2019 Crystal Odom

First paperback edition May 2019

Book design by Jake Odom
Text is set in Sabon LT Pro.

ISBN 9781798856659 (paperback)

Published by Kindle Direct Publishing
Kdp.amazon.com

First Edition
First Edition: May 2019

This paperback edition first published in 2019

Visit the author's website at
CrystalOdom.com

Facing Goliath

A JOURNEY OF HOPE

Crystal Odom

for Jack

Facing Goliath

A JOURNEY OF HOPE

Crystal Odom

Introduction

When I was a kid, my mom used to say that I danced to the beat of my own drum. I think that was her loving-mom way of saying that I was quirky. I totally and completely owned the fact that I liked to do life a little bit off the beaten path. But then, when I was nine years old my parents got divorced and it left a crack deep down inside of me that nothing could ever completely fill. Because of that crack, I grew into this deep and profound longing for what I thought was "normal." Back then, I thought normal was a family that lived on a street where all of the houses looked the same with a mom who drove an SUV to drop her kids off at soccer practice. And for many years of my life, that was the happily ever after I was searching for.

But the truth is, there is no such thing as "normal." Everyone has a story to tell. Whether you've been through a lot of really awful, hard stuff or you've had an easy breezy life so far… your story is your story. And the Bible is pretty clear on the fact that we will ALL experience difficult times. In fact, in John 16:33 Jesus tells his friends that "in this world you WILL have trouble… " He doesn't say you might experience some hard times. No friends. He says YOU WILL. And boy did they. But that's a different story for a different day. Right now, I want to introduce you to my story. No. Actually, I want to introduce you to our story. Because this book isn't just about me and the tough things I've been through. It's about my oldest son, Jack and all of the insanely difficult ways that God used him to change my the world.

I have often said that if God himself had knocked on my front door and asked me if I would do this one thing for Him... If He had stood there in my doorway with bright beaming light shining all around Him and said that I could make a real impact for His kingdom and all it would cost me was my firstborn son's health... I feel quite certain I would have said, "no thank you." I mean, it's certainly not that I don't want to make an impact for the kingdom. I do. I really do. But y'all. I'm no Abraham. And so I believe that since God knew that the thing I was going to have to do would be the hardest thing... He didn't give me a choice. Instead, He allowed it to be placed in my path and then gave me ALL THE GRACE that I could ever need to move through it day by day. And y'all, when life gives you lemons, there's only one thing you can do.

Jack Aaron Odom was the answer to a lifetime of prayers. The boy who made me a mom. The first cry that brought purpose and meaning into my world like I had never even known existed before that moment. Beautiful and perfect on the outside. Broken heart on the inside. Becoming a parent for the first time (or anytime at all) is a spiritual experience. One of the few moments in your life when everything completely changes in a single moment. The day that I became a mom, my life changed forever. But not just in the normal new-mom life-changing way. My life turned upside down when I was told that my son was born with "half a heart." We were told that in order to live he would have to undergo a series of major open-heart surgeries and would face a lifetime of medical treatment. The surgeries would keep him alive, but they would not fix his heart. Only treat the symptoms and allow him time that he would otherwise not be given. We were told that his future was not promised or clear. There were countless unanswered questions.

This book is a record of our journey. I wrote each entry as we were facing each different step along the way and have compiled all of those entries here into one collection. A string of events, ups and downs, very good days and very bad days, that together form one simple story of a life that was created with purpose and meaning. I don't dare say that our story is more difficult than others. I fully recognize how blessed we are that our son is still here, healthy and alive, while so many others have not been as fortunate. And for that reason, I ask you not to come into this story with any type of comparison in mind. I work truly very hard not to compare my own journey with others' and I ask you to do the same. For some, our story will seem like a mountain you could never imagine having to climb. It will pull at your heartstrings and send you in to your kids' bedrooms long after they've gone to sleep for the night to give one last kiss goodnight and to send up a "thank you Lord" for the health that you've taken for granted. To you, I want to say this: kiss them once for me. And don't you EVER feel bad for one single second that God blessed you with healthy babies. They have a story all their own. Teach them Jesus and help them find their purpose. For others, it will seem like a molehill for which you would gladly trade with your own story. Your mountains cast shadows that completely envelope the story that I am telling. To you, my friend, I am so very sorry for the hand that this life has dealt you. And I hope that in some way, this story can bring you some comfort in the form of a reminder that though our battles are different, our fight is the same. You are strong. You are brave. And most importantly, my friend, you are not alone.

PART 1

THE GLENN

SUNDAY, FEBRUARY 5, 2012

Expecting

<hr>

"Before I formed you in the womb I knew you,
before you were born I set you apart…"
JEREMIAH 1:5

I always knew that I wanted to be a mom someday. I was the kind of kid who loved to take care of other kids. I think I was just born with that maternal instinct. I guess in a lot of ways that's probably why I became a teacher too. But Josh and I got married young. I was 21 and he was only 18. (If I had a dollar for every time someone called me a cradle robber…) At that time in our lives, we were still just kids trying to figure out how to be adults and how to be married and how to pay the bills (that last one was a real struggle back in the day.) So we knew it was best if we waited a few years before we started a family. So we did. We spent the next 4+ years learning, growing, laughing, fighting and figuring out our life. Marriage is tough, y'all. And I'll be honest… Ours almost didn't survive those first four years. But that's a different story for a different day…

In December of 2010, I graduated from college. Praise the Lord FOR REAL on that one because it was TOUGH. But it was a milestone we had been waiting for. It meant that we were finally going to be able to feel settled. Josh had been working for a big Fortune 500 company for a few years already and I was about to become a teacher. Life was beginning to feel more adult-ish.

In December of that year, we went on a vacation with some friends to the mountains. They had the cutest little boy who was around two-years-old at the time. We spent the week loving on him and carrying him around, secretly wondering what it would be like to have one of our own. So one night while we were still on that trip we sat down on the bed and talked about it. And right then and there we decided it was time to grow our family.

MAY 11, 2011

I had been having some weird feeling stomach cramps. I just thought mother nature was headed my way.

After a couple of weeks with no change and no sign of mother nature to be found, I got curious. I stopped at Dollar General on the way to work and picked up a generic pregnancy test. I didn't even give it much thought. I knew it would be negative and I didn't want to get my hopes up. I had taken so many pregnancy tests since we decided to start trying to get pregnant and I was always disappointed when they were negative.

I threw the test in my purse and went to work.

That night when I got home from work at around 10:30, I told Josh how I had been feeling. I told him that I was sure I wasn't pregnant. Then I told him I knew how we could know for sure. I told him about the test in my purse and he told me to take it right then. I could tell he got excited but I was just sure it would be negative. I had done this a thousand times before.

I took the test and left it lying on the bathroom counter. I went back a few minutes later to look at the test and it was a very faded plus sign. I was more confused than anything. I mean, after all, it did come from Dollar General. I told Josh to come look. We just looked at each other for a while. He asked me if it had ever looked like that before. I said nope.

We jumped up right then and ran to Walmart, full of potential excitement. We were trying not to get our hopes up. We were really nervous. Josh drove like a maniac. We talked the entire way there. A thousand "what ifs" hung in the air all around us.

When we got there, it was around midnight and there was another couple standing in front of the section. We were looking at pregnancy tests and they were buying preventative products. We chose the tests that were in a plastic box that would have to be removed at the register. They were the most expensive, but we wanted to be sure.

When we got to the register, there was only one aisle open and a couple of people behind us. As the checkout lady tried to open the plastic box, she got frustrated and then called loudly for her manager to come help her open a pregnancy test for "these kids." We laughed as the older ladies behind us looked us up and down. We joked that it didn't help that we both looked like we were about 17. Josh even joked that he should pretend to call his mom and tell her we were ready to be picked up from Walmart.

We rushed home and I went straight to the bathroom. I had bought a bottle of water at Walmart and Josh forced me to drink some of it so that I would have to pee when I got home. I took both tests at one time and was really pretty sure that I didn't pee enough on either for them to work.

I left the tests on the counter in the bathroom and sat on the edge of our bed with Josh. We closed our eyes, bowed our heads, held hands, and prayed for God's will. If it was time for us to have a baby, we wanted it to be positive. We wanted whatever He had in store for us. We both prayed so hard for His will.

Nothing more. Nothing less.

When a few minutes had passed and we were done praying, I asked Josh to let me look. He waited on the bed. I stood at the bathroom counter in total shock when I walked in and saw TWO words. PREGNANT. PREGNANT.

I didn't say anything. I didn't move. I always knew it would happen someday but I had been dreaming of that moment for years. How we would react. How we would celebrate. It was so surreal.

I stepped out of the bathroom and just looked at Josh. I didn't say anything. He asked, "Well?" I didn't say anything.

I shook my head. He was shocked too. Had to see it for himself. He came into the bathroom. We both just stared at the tests like we were expecting them to change.

After a few moments, we started to laugh together. Then cry together. We hugged for the longest time. He held onto me so tight. He was crying. I was overwhelmed with emotion. We laughed and cried together in that tiny bathroom.

2011 was an incredibly difficult year for me on a personal level. Getting pregnant only amplified my emotions. I was happy, of course, but I was also scared. I had no idea what God was doing in my life or why I was experiencing the things I was experiencing. Now, when I look back on that year I can see God's hand ALL OVER every single moment. I can see His grace pouring over me in even the deepest of my sorrows. Back then, I think there were times when I felt abandoned by God. I questioned Him. I was angry with Him. But if only I had known how He was growing me and preparing my heart for what was about to take place in my life.

TUESDAY, FEBRUARY 14, 2012

Delivery Dilemma

"If any of you lacks wisdom, you should ask God, who gives generously to all without finding fault, and it will be given to you."

JAMES 1:5

We made each of our weekly visits to the doctor's office during the last few weeks of my pregnancy with our fingers crossed, hoping for good news. Each week, we were told that nothing had changed. I wasn't dilating at all. We made our last visit on January 10th. I was 40 weeks and 1 day pregnant and was scheduled for an ultrasound. My doctor wanted to check and make sure everything looked good with the baby before scheduling an induction for later that week.

During the ultrasound we were told that our baby was likely going to weigh 9 pounds and 9 ounces. We were shocked! That's a big baby! After the ultrasound we went for a non-stress test. We sat in a tiny room for 30 minutes, just me and Josh. I was hooked up to some monitors and I had to push a button every time I felt the baby move. We sat there and talked and laughed about the possibility of having such a big baby. I was nervous about delivering already but now it was just amplified! We texted and told our families. We wondered what the doctor was going to say.

After the non-stress test we saw the doctor. She told us that she was positive, judging by the size and shape of my belly that this baby was not going to be that large, but she also added that she had been wrong before. She gave us the option. We could either try to have a regular delivery or go ahead and schedule a C-section. If we chose a regular delivery the plan was going to be to come in on Thursday night and they would give me some medicine that would prepare me to be induced the next morning. Then they would induce Friday morning. However, because I hadn't dilated at all, there was a chance that I could labor for hours and still not be able to push out such a large baby. This actually happened to my mom when my older sister was born. She labored for a very long time and ended up being too small to have such a large baby. She had to have an emergency C-section anyway and had been through many hours of torturous pain for nothing. I guess that's the literal meaning of the phrase "laboring in vain." I was really scared the same thing would happen to me.

The worst part was that she told us that we had to decide right then. The longer we waited to make the decision, the longer we would have to wait to have our baby. Josh held my hand as I told her I wanted to have a C-section. As soon as she left the room I fell to pieces. I was terrified of having surgery. I had seen that operating room. It was really bright, cold, and scary. Josh hugged me and reassured me that everything was going to be fine.

Later that day, after we had made it home and just sat down to have lunch, my phone rang. It was the scheduling office calling to tell me when my C-section was going to be... a.k.a. when we were going to become parents. He told us that he had scheduled my surgery for 1:00 the next afternoon. We were so excited that we couldn't even finish our lunch. We started calling our families to let them know. Tomorrow was the big day.

That night we packed and got everything ready. We couldn't wrap our minds around the fact that this time tomorrow our baby would be here. After all these months, it was finally time. The day I had waited my whole life for. The day that would change my life forever. We were so ready.

This day to us was just another doctor's visit. It was both exciting and scary. Exciting because we found out that our baby boy was going to come into the world the next day. Scary because we found out that he was going to get here via gaping hole in Mommy's belly.

We were just getting ready for what was to come. We thought we were making the decision about the delivery based on what would be the least painful and dangerous route for me and baby. Little did we know that God was there the whole time. And that I didn't really make that decision about the C-section at all. God did.

Welcome to the World Baby Jack

"For I know the plans I have for you," declares the LORD, "plans to prosper you and not to harm you, plans to give you hope and a future."

JEREMIAH 29:11

I don't think either one of us did much sleeping that night. We were SO excited. Our baby was finally going to be here.

We got up that morning and got ready then we finished packing. My mom came over and we had so much luggage that we literally filled up two cars. You would have thought we were moving into the hospital and the funny thing was that we were only planning to be there three nights (although we ended up being there longer and eventually ran out of stuff and had to send our family to get more stuff for us.) We left home at around 9:30am because Josh and I had to go through the bank drive-thru

We got to the hospital right at 11:00am. We went to the third floor and checked in. A sweet nurse named Erica took us to our room and gave me my gown. I got dressed and got into the bed. She asked me a bunch of questions and then started my IV (My very first one ever/ I was SO nervous/ It didn't hurt that bad.) After that it was just a waiting game. I was scheduled for surgery at 1:00pm and Erica said she would be back to get me at around a quarter til.

Our families started to arrive little by little until our little hospital room was filled to the max. I watched the clock like a hawk, commenting every few minutes. ("20 minutes til they cut me open/10 minutes and they're coming to get me") Needless to say I was all nerves. Every time Erica came into the room I panicked. She would say, "Not yet. Try to relax."

Then it was time. 12:45pm. She came into the room.

"Are you ready?" She asked.

"Yes," is what I said. "Aahhh!" is what I felt.

Josh got suited up in his wicked cool surgery gear. I got a lovely hat and then they wrapped me up in a sheet, grabbed my IV fluids, and off we went. Our families lined the hallway to watch us walk down to the OR. I was shaking like a leaf. I had never been so terrified and excited before in my life.

When we got down there, they told me that Josh had to stay outside of the OR while they prepped me for surgery. I seriously hoped they were kidding. They weren't.

I went into that icy cold and ridiculously bright room by myself. Time to put on my brave face. One last look over my shoulder to my sweet husband. I was on my own, at least for a little while.

When we got in there, I met the anesthesiologist and he explained what was going to happen. First they would have me sit on the table and lean forward while they gave me an epidural. Then I would quickly lie down on the table and get situated before I started to lose feeling in the lower half of my body. Then they would begin the process of prepping me, which included a lot of things I would rather not share.

I loved that Erica was in there with me and she held my hands while I got my epidural. I had been really nervous about that part and she could tell. She told me to try to relax because they needed for me to stop shaking. She asked me questions about the baby. I calmed down. Then a small prick in my back. A LOT of intense burning for a couple of seconds. Then the second prick. A LOT of pressure. Then done. I survived. They said I took it like a champ. I was sad that Josh and my family didn't get to see me being all brave. (Mental note, make sure Erica tells Josh how tough I was.)

While the doctors prepped me, the anesthesiologist hung all of the draping that would keep me from being able to see what they were doing to me. The anesthesiologist had explained to me that my blood pressure would probably drop and it might make me nauseated or light headed. I had to tell them immediately if that happened. It definitely did. I suddenly got intensely nauseated and dizzy. He pushed something into my IV and I was instantly better. I told him that was a miracle drug and I wanted to take some home. Then my doctor said that she was ready. "Bring in dad," she said. Then Josh was finally by my side. He sat on a stool on the left side of me, up by my head. My arms were under the draping laying out to each side. I wasn't supposed to move them. But Josh reached under to hold my hand.

They did a lot of poking to make sure I couldn't feel anything and then the anesthesiologist explained how the pressure was going to feel like my doctor was standing on my stomach, then my chest. I wondered what that would feel like. Then they said it was time. "Are you ready?" They asked me.

I wasn't scared anymore. I had survived my first IV and my epidural. I had been in this cold creepy room with all of these strangers for long enough to feel like we were all old pals. I was more ready than I'd ever been for anything in my entire life. I was dying to see my baby's face. "So ready," I answered.

So then they began. The anesthesiologist explained everything they were doing step by step. Once they got in there, the baby was stuck. He didn't want to come out. The doctor explained that she was going to have to cut me wider to be able to reach him. He was much farther up than they had anticipated. Then she explained that they were going to have to use the vacuum to try to get him out. We heard it pop three times. That was the sound of the suction cup popping off of my stubborn boy's little head as he remained comfortably situated just high enough to be unreachable. Then the doctor said it was time for that pressure they had talked about, and it might be worse than they had originally let on.

Sure enough, the doctor definitely placed a rather large elephant on my chest. I couldn't see it, but I'm definitely sure that it was there. I couldn't breathe. Josh squeezed my hand and told me that it would be over soon. "You can do this. It's ok. You're doing great. I'm so proud of you." Seemed like that moment lasted forever. It was intense to say the least. Suddenly a spray of blood hit the drape that was hanging in front of my face. It sprayed onto the anesthesiologist and the wall behind him. Not cool.

"More pressure," the doctor said.

"They're kidding, right?" I thought to myself but couldn't speak because suddenly the elephant decided to invite his buddy to hop on. I felt like my chest was caving in. That definitely has to be what it feels like to be squished between two walls like in horror movies when the walls start to close in and the people that are trapped get their guts squished out. Yuck. Not fun.

Then the doctor asked Josh if he wanted to watch. She was about to pull the baby out. It was finally time. Josh stood up. More pressure. Then he was out.

I watched Josh's face as I waited to hear the first cry of my newborn son. He was definitely amazed. Then, there it was. The most beautiful, amazing sound I had ever heard. I couldn't see him. But I could hear him. My tears began to fall rapidly, but since I wasn't allowed to move my arms, Josh did his best to wipe my face.

The nurse said that they had to do a few things and then they would bring him over. The doctor said that she was going to start closing me back up. The anesthesiologist said that he was a big healthy boy. He asked if we wanted to guess a weight. I said 9 pounds 2 ounces. Josh said 9.4. The anesthesiologist guessed 9.14. We were all wrong.

"Eight pounds, eight ounces," the nurse said.

"I was way off," the anesthesiologist said.

Then it was finally time. The moment I had waited for. The nurse brought him over. He was bundled up in a hospital blanket. She held him out for me to see.

Cue all the tears "He's perfect," was all I could say.

The first thing I noticed were his sweet little lips. His little mouth was all puckered out. And he had hair! We totally thought he would be bald. A sweet little round head of strawberry blonde hair. He was screaming bloody murder.

Then she took him back. They still had lots to do. He screamed the whole time. The doctors commented on his strong lungs.

Josh and I cried together and talked about how amazingly perfect he was. He was so much better than I could have possibly imagined. It was the most amazing and beautiful moment of my life. I wish it could have lasted forever.

Then finally the nurse brought him back and handed him to his proud daddy. Josh took him into his arms and we both stared at him in amazement. He was the most beautiful thing we had ever seen. The anesthesiologist took our camera and took some pictures. Then finally, after what felt like a century, The doctor said she was done. They took down all of the draping and moved me onto a hospital bed. They got me situated and then Erica took the baby from Josh and placed him in my arms.

It was one of those moments that defines your life. The moment you accepted the Lord as your savior. The moment you said, "I do" and became a Mrs. And now this. The moment you make eye contact with the small person who had been growing inside of you for nine long months and who had instantly become the love of your life. The moment you became a mother. The moment you realized that you didn't even know what love was until now.

SATURDAY, FEBRUARY 25, 2012

Something's Wrong
With His Heart

"When you pass through the waters, I will be with you; and when you pass
through the rivers, they will not sweep over you. When you walk through
the fire, you will not be burned; the flames will not set you ablaze."

ISAIAH 43:2

So they put my sweet baby boy into my arms for the first
time and wheeled us out of the OR. My eyes were fixed on his
precious face. I studied his tiny features as we made our way
back to our room. When we turned the corner I could see that
the hallway outside of our room was packed with our family,
lining the walls with cameras ready, like a mob of paparazzi.

As soon as we got back into our room, they took the baby
from me. They allowed our family into the room for a few minutes while they got him situated across the room from me. Our
whole family crowded around him until the room was so packed
that I couldn't see him anymore. I watched their faces as they
met him for the first time.

Then the nurses asked our family to clear out of the room
and reassured them that they could all come back soon. When
the room was empty one of the nurses was suctioning fluid out
of the baby's mouth. He would cry, then cough, then cry again.
She explained to me that he had a lot of fluid that still needed

to come out and that because of that fluid, his breathing wasn't quite up to par.

"Nothing to worry about," she said. "Happens all the time."

She hooked him up to a little machine that measured his oxygen saturation. She said it was low. I didn't know what that meant. They explained to me that the number on the screen should be around 90 and his was sitting right at 70. She told me that she had to call the NICU and ask the doctor if they wanted him to come down there for a while. I heard her on the phone asking him if the baby could stay in our room. He said no. They were coming to get him.

I started to cry. I didn't understand what was happening. He was just born a few minutes ago. It was all happening really fast. This was not at all how I pictured this day. I was supposed to be trying to nurse for the first time and then my family was supposed to come back so that we could all stare at him in adoration for several hours. Now they were taking him from me and I wouldn't see him for four whole hours?

What were they going to do to him? Why couldn't I go? Was he going to be okay?

Our nurse Erica came over and told me not to worry. She told me that this happens often with C-section babies because they don't have to do any work to get out. She said it causes them to retain fluid in their lungs. She told me that they would keep him in the NICU for a four hour observation then they would bring him back to me.

The NICU people came into the room with one of those awful covered incubators. They asked if I wanted to hold him again for a few minutes before they took him. Of course I said yes. The few minutes passed much too quickly, then they took him from me and put him in that glass box. I cried. They said he was blue and that scared me. Then they took him down to the

NICU. Josh kissed me, told me that the baby was going to be fine, then followed them down there.

Then it was just me and Erica in the room. I was overwhelmed and really confused about what was wrong with him.

Was it serious?

"Don't worry," she said. "It's not like he's going to die or anything. He'll be fine."

It seemed like a really harsh thing for her to say but truthfully, it was exactly what I needed to hear. I was a brand new mommy who had just met my baby only minutes ago. Then had him ripped from my arms and hauled off in a glass box surrounded by doctors that were all saying things I didn't understand. It was terrifying.

Once they were gone and I had been pumped full of drugs to prepare me for the feeling to come back, which was going to be seriously painful, they allowed our family to come back into the room with me.

For anyone who has ever had major abdominal surgery, you understand that no amount of pain medicine could ever be enough when the feeling first comes back. It hurt. A lot. The feeling came back as I waited to hear from Josh. It was also a moment of heavy emotion for me. I cried a lot. This made the pain worse. Then I cried more because it hurt so bad. It was a catch-22 cycle of pain and tears.

After a while of waiting, I started to worry. I knew my husband and I knew that too much time had passed. I tried calling him. No answer. I tried texting him. No response. Something was wrong. I could feel it. I knew he would have called me by now. He knows how I worry.

Our family had gone back out into the waiting area and it was just my mom and me in my room when Josh came back in. He was out of breath. He had ran back to me. The moment that he came around the corner and I saw his face, I knew something was wrong. He was scared.

He sat down on the bed next to me and took my hands. Tears welled in his eyes. He tried to choke them back. He wanted to be strong for me.

"What is it? Tell me what's wrong. Tell me right now!" I said as my heart thudded in my chest. It seemed like a century before he spoke.

"Something's wrong with his heart."

He broke down. Tears fell.

I didn't understand. The room was spinning. I was sure he was wrong. This wasn't happening. It wasn't real. It was the most intense out of body experience I have ever experienced. I wanted him to take it back. To say it wasn't true. I just didn't understand how this was possible. Was he going to die? I was in shock.

My mom left the room to give us a moment. The rest of that moment was private and highly emotional. I won't share all of the details with you but I will say that it was the hardest moment of my life up until that point.

In that time Josh shared with me what the nurses and doctors in the NICU had told him. When they brought Jack down to monitor his oxygen saturation, they hooked him up to monitors. While one of the nurses was sitting close by, she heard what sounded like a heart murmur. She called the doctor who then called UAB. They knew there was a problem with his heart but at that point they had no idea what that problem was or how serious. They were going to transfer him to the NICU at UAB to have some tests run. The ambulance would take him there at 8:00pm. We would know more in the morning.

Soon enough our family filled the room. They wanted to be there for us but no one knew what to say.

I decided right then that I was going to him. I wasn't going to lie in that hospital bed not knowing what was going on. Not knowing what they were doing to my baby. He needed me. I didn't care what anyone said. I was going.

My nurse brought me a wheelchair. Getting out of the bed and into that wheelchair only a little over an hour after my surgery was pretty rough to say the least. Once I got situated, they put a blanket in my lap and she wheeled me down to the NICU.

She was a horrible driver. It was intensely painful. She hit every bump without hesitation and even ran me into the baby's incubator when we got down there. I don't think I'll ever forget that ride.

Once we got down there they situated me in my wheelchair right in front of the baby. He was already hooked up to all kinds of monitors and had tiny IVs in both tiny hands.

The nurse asked if I wanted to hold him. I said yes, of course. She bundled him up and handed him to me. For the next few hours, I sat in that wheelchair, holding my new son, speaking scripture over him and begging God for mercy.

"Please God. Let him be okay. Please."

Josh stayed at my side. My dad and my mom took turns holding a wet cloth on the back of my neck and pushing my hair out of my face. The rest of our family members took turns standing in the room with us. We said several prayers together.

Looking back now, that evening is a blur. I don't think I saw anything but his tiny face for hours. Since then we've seen some videos and pictures that were taken in that room during that time and I don't even remember seeing most of the people that were there. It was a time of intense emotion and close connection to God. He was in that room with us. I have no doubt about that.

As 8:00 drew near, I got nervous. They were going to take

him and Josh was going with him. It was the most devastating feeling to know that I couldn't be there with him. He needed me. Josh needed me. I felt so helpless.

They chose a nurse who would ride in the ambulance with him. She assured me that she would take good care of him. They took him from me and placed him back in the incubator. We prayed one more time and then I said my tearful goodbyes to Jack and to Josh. It was harder than I could ever explain.

We followed them down the hallway as far as they would let us but then they told us that I had to go back to my room. They wouldn't let me go any further. I watched them until they were out of my sight. Then they took me back to my room.

As for the rest of that night, I'll be honest, I don't remember much. I remember some visitors but by the end of the night, it was just me and my mom. She spent the night on the couch in my room. She helped me whenever I needed to make those dreaded trips to the bathroom. Of course, I didn't sleep. The first night was bad. I stayed in constant contact with Josh and he sent me videos and pictures every few minutes. I was in a lot of pain, both physically and emotionally. I spent a lot of time in prayer. The room was dark and silent. I just talked to God.

The purpose of sharing this part of our story with you is, by no means, to bum you out. It's actually quite the opposite. I want to remind you that God is good. He wants the very best for us and He understands what is ultimately best for us even when we do not. God loves us more than we could ever comprehend and that love He has for us transcends this world and the moment we are living in. He was with us throughout this tough day and He is with us still. Jack has defied every odd and has won every battle he has faced so far and I know that he will continue to do so as we proceed into the future. God has a purpose. He has a plan. We have 100% faith in His plan and we will walk through the fire because we know that our victory awaits us on the other side. We WILL watch our little boy grow up into a strong man of God and in 30 years we will look back on this day and we will know exactly what God's plan was all along and we will celebrate any and every opportunity that God allowed each of us to be used for His glory.

> "Our light and momentary troubles are achieving for us
> an eternal glory that far outweighs them all."
>
> 2 CORINTHIANS 4:17

Congenital Heart Disease

"Now to him who is able to do immeasurably more than all we ask
or imagine, according to his power that is at work within us."

EPHESIANS 3:20

JACK'S DIAGNOSIS

The first night was hard. Jack had been transferred to UAB and I was still at St. Vincent's. That night they told us that they would do some tests in the morning and then we would know more. I can't begin to describe what it felt like to be separated from him and Josh in that scary time. It was only by the grace of God that I made it through.

The next day it seemed like a lifetime passed before we finally heard from the doctor. I stayed in constant contact with Josh that morning. I sat helpless, feeling a million miles away in my hospital bed, waiting... and praying.

Finally after 1:00 in the afternoon, the cardiologist, Dr. Law came in to talk to Josh and the rest of our family.

I texted Josh during that time and he told me that the doctor was in there explaining everything to them and he would call me as soon as the doctor left.

I told my mom and my sister who were in my room with me and we prayed together. I spent the remainder of that time praying and speaking scripture. I was terrified but doing my best to put my faith in God and trust that good news was coming. It seemed like years passed before Josh called. When the phone finally rang, I thought that my heart was going to leap out of my chest. It was one of the most serious moments of my life.

Josh explained to me what Dr. Law had just explained to him. At the time it was a lot of information and it was confusing and scary. Since then I have had plenty of time to study Jack's condition and grow more comfortable with the terminology.

Here is everything Dr. Law explained to Josh and our family that day. It's precise in detail because they videoed him speaking and I wrote it all down straight from the video. It's complicated, but pretty much explains it all in good detail. Here it is.

Jack's heart is built different from a normal heart. First of all, there is no way for blood to go from the left atrium to the left ventricle because the valve that separates the two chambers didn't form. This is called Mitral Atresia. So, in Jack's heart, blood is having to take a longer route to get from the lungs back into the heart and back out into the body. Also when this blood is coming back into the heart it can go one of two places. It can go across the pulmonary valve or into the aorta because there is a hole between the bottom chambers of the heart (the right ventricle and the left ventricle.) This is called a Ventricular Septal Defect or VSD.

They are not able to make Jack's heart into a normal heart, but they have ways to treat his heart as it is. They will have to re-route the blood flow as time goes by. This is because the left ventricle is too small and also because the valve that separates the left atrium and left ventricle didn't form.

There's more but we'll come back to that later.

At the time, Jack was on a medicine called prostaglandins which was being administered through an IV. This medicine was keeping his Patent Ductus Arteriosus or PDA open. All babies are born with their PDA open which allows blood to flow between the pulmonary valve and the aorta. In normal babies, the PDA closes within the first few days of life. They needed to keep that open in Jack's heart for now with the prostaglandins. This was ensuring that there was enough blood flow going to his lungs.

At this time, the first question that needed to be answered was whether or not Jack needed the PDA to remain open. If the PDA closed and he was still getting a sufficient amount of blood flow to the lungs then he didn't really need it to remain open. Even in Jack's heart, blood could get out into the lungs from the heart, however, his pulmonary valve was a little bit smaller and had a narrowing at the opening (called Pulmonary Stenosis) which would make it more difficult for blood to flow through, leaving his cardiologist to wonder if the amount of blood that could flow through there would be enough. The question he didn't know the answer to at that time was if it was too small or too narrow and he couldn't tell that while the PDA was still open.

So, what he recommended was that the RNICU doctors turn off the prostaglandins at 6am the next morning. The reason why he wanted to wait until the next day was that sometimes turning off the medicine could create an emergent situation (like if they turn it off and Jack's body wasn't getting enough blood to his lungs on his own.) In that case, those doctors would have to decide what to do. The RNICU doctors were not cardiologists, nor did they know Jack's case particularly well. So, Dr. Law, Jack's cardiologist, wanted to wait until the next morning when he would be there in case they needed him. It was just safer and easier for everyone that way.

They needed to take this step (turning off the prostaglandins and allowing the PDA to close) so that they could see if there was enough blood flow to the lungs without the medicine because Jack couldn't stay in the RNICU forever on the medicine. They had to figure out how to ensure that he was getting enough blood flow. They would turn it off and see how his oxygen saturation looked over the next few days as the PDA closed. They explained to us that an acceptable oxygen saturation was usually in the 80s.

If they turn off the prostaglandins and allow the PDA to close and there is enough blood flow to the lungs to keep his oxygen levels in the 80s on his own without the PDA then he would get to go home. We would follow up closely with the cardiologist in the pediatric cardiology clinic at UAB over the next few months. If they allow the PDA to close and his oxygen levels begin to drop, he would require an immediate open-heart surgery to fix that problem before we could leave the hospital with him.

This surgery, called the Norwood Procedure, would consist of placing a shunt in his heart to allow a sufficient amount of blood to flow to the lungs. Basically they would replace the PDA with another tube that connected blood flow from the pulmonary artery to the aorta.

Either way, whether he needed the first surgery or not, Jack would be sent home to grow over the next few months. Then in approximately three to six months he would need the next surgery.

If he didn't have to have the first procedure, then he would have a heart cath before the second and third surgeries in the series. The cath would tell the doctors if the pressure or resistance in the lung arteries is high, if it is high then the second surgery will not work. Dr. Law said that he didn't feel like that would be a problem but they have to check anyway.

The next open-heart surgery in the series is called a Bidirectional Glenn. Jack would be put on pulmonary bypass for this procedure. This surgery would connect the blood that comes into the heart from the head and arms (blood from the superior vena cava) into the pulmonary artery (lung artery). This allows the blue blood that comes from the head and arms to go into and back out of the lungs.

After this surgery, Jack would be sent home to grow again. The only issue after the first surgery will be that there is still some blue blood going out to the rest of his body and his oxygen levels still wouldn't be normal. So after he has had a few years to grow they would perform a final procedure called the Fontan procedure.

There isn't a specific time frame for the Fontan procedure. They usually perform it at around 2–5 years of age. Dr. Law said that we (Jack's parents) would be the ones who would dictate when Jack's surgery would be based on his endurance levels and coloring. He said once Jack starts running and playing as he gets bigger, he would begin to lose endurance and start to lose some of the pinking in his color. (i.e. he would turn blue and lose his breath easily.) When that starts to happen to him, whether he is 2 or 5, that will be the time when he needs the surgery. Even if it doesn't happen to him within those years, they wouldn't allow him to go past the age of 5 because they think it's good to get the surgeries over with while they are young enough that they don't remember them when they are older.

In the Fontan procedure they would take the blood that comes from the lower part of the body and route it into the lung artery. (This would connect the inferior vena cava to the pulmonary artery.) Then after these surgeries his oxygen levels would be close to normal.

There wouldn't be any more necessary surgeries or interventions required. He will require lifelong cardiology follow-up and will be watched closely throughout his life in the cardiology clinic. He will go onto live his life but will be challenged in areas of stamina and endurance. Dr. Law joked that Jack probably won't be a star athlete but neither was he and he turned out just fine.

To sum it all up, Jack has a condition called Double Inlet Left Ventricle, sometimes referred to as Single Ventricle. Mitral Atresia, VSD, and Pulmonary Stenosis are all covered under that main term of Single Ventricle.

Dr. Law said that many children go through these procedures and do really well after the surgeries. He can't guarantee that Jack won't need a heart transplant one day but he wants to just focus on what is immediately in front of us right now. He said there is no way to know what he will need in 20–30 years but for now he thinks that Jack will do well with these procedures. He said that Jack is going to have to go through a lot and every step has risks, but he thinks Jack is in a low-risk category for most everything at this point in time.

To make a long story a little bit longer…

The next morning at 6am I was up, showered and ready to go. I was closely monitoring what was going on with Jack via texting with Josh while I waited for my doctor to come by and sign my discharge papers. I was on pins and needles waiting to get out of that place. When she finally came by, she gave me a quick once-over and set me free. We got to UAB in one minute flat.

My mom and sister dropped me off at the door where Josh was waiting with a wheelchair and they went to find a pharmacy to fill my prescriptions. We couldn't get up to the RNICU fast enough. I was dying to see my baby again. It had been two long days and a lot of tears since I handed him to that nurse.

When I finally got to him, my heart melted. He was sleeping so sweetly, all bundled up on a tiny little NICU bed. I burst into tears. Josh held me as I cried and let out every emotion that I had been feeling for two days. The nurse came in and wrapped up all of his little cords and finally handed him to me. It was the most glorious moment. I was finally holding my sweet boy again, something that, for a time, I was scared I might never get to do again. Tears streamed down my face as I held him and stared into his sweet little face. My boy. Mommy's boy.

Later that day Dr. Law, the cardiologist, came by to see me and ask if I had any questions. Of course I had hundreds but none that I was emotionally ready to face. That day I just wanted to hold my boy and forget that his heart was sick. I held him in that chair all day long. I finally got the chance to feed him for the first time. I won't go into detail about how a male nurse helped me learn how to breastfeed for the first time. To sum it up, I made it nice and awkward for both of us.

Throughout that day, the nurses came in to check on us and I got acquainted with my new hospital home. The RNICU at UAB is amazing. Every baby has their own little private room with a chair and a couch. Josh and I never had to leave his side for the remainder of our stay. I am eternally grateful for that and for the sweet demeanor of the nursing staff that worked with us that week. They loved Jack too and were rooting for him with us. I'll never forget them.

Over the next few days we watched Jack's monitor like there was an award winning movie playing on that screen. Every time he moved it beeped and every time it beeped I panicked and every time I panicked I called for a nurse and every time a nurse came they had to reassure me that he was fine. It was a never ending cycle of me making sure those poor nurses were having to work for their pay. They probably weren't too sad to see us go.

The good amazing news was that Jack's oxygen saturation

level never dropped. It stayed in the high 70s to low 80s the remainder of the week. And after only 6 days in the RNICU, they told us we were going to get to go home. Jack didn't need the first surgery. He was doing just fine on his own. When the doctor came in the morning of the 17th to tell us that Jack's ECHO showed that his PDA was completely closed and he was maintaining enough blood flow on his own to keep his oxygen levels up, I cried like a baby. It was another one of those wonderful moments that God allowed us to truly see Him working in Jack's little body. He had worked another miracle and we were overwhelmed with joy that we were going to get to take him home that day.

Later that day, after waiting about 8 hours for one shot that Jack had to have, we were finally discharged. We packed up everything we had brought and our families had brought to us, which basically looked like we were moving, and we dressed Jack in his sweet little going home outfit. They finally removed all of his cords and wires and he was completely free for the first time in his little life. The nurse made me get back into a wheelchair even though I had been walking around there for nearly a week just fine, then she handed me my baby and wheeled me out to the car. We loaded our little bundle of joy into his car seat for the first time, and then we took him home.

There are many stories I could share with you about our week in the RNICU. Some amazing moments of joy, some moments of fear and even terror, and some moments where we truly felt the peace of God settle in the room with us. For now, it's just important for you to know that we experienced our first real victory that week. God allowed Jack's body to perform a miraculous task which he is still performing right now. He is breathing on his own thanks to an adequate supply of blood flow to his lungs. Something that his doctor wasn't sure he would be able to do because of the combination of heart defects that he was born with.

God has done so much for my sweet boy in his short two and a half months of life. That first week was the beginning of an amazing show of God's power. God is still a miracle worker and if you ever doubt that, just look at my sweet son. If it weren't for a nurse telling me that Jack was going to weigh over a pound more than he actually weighed I wouldn't have chosen to have a C-section. If I hadn't had a C-section Jack could have died during childbirth because his little heart might not have been able to take the stress. Then also if it weren't for a nurse noticing his trouble breathing and then another nurse hearing his heart murmur while in the same room, they might not have found his heart problems and he would have died within a few months without any explanation. This is the absolute show of God's miracle working power. I'm not sure what God's plan is for Jack but I know He has a BIG one. I am certain that Jack is going to grow into a strong man of God and is going to do great things for the kingdom of God.

TUESDAY, APRIL 10, 2012

Easter and a Heart Cath

"And those who know your name put their trust in you, for you,
O Lord, have not forsaken those who seek you."

PSALM 9:10

Tomorrow is Baby Jack's three months birthday! Happy birthday Baby Jack!

Thinking back to just three short months ago… I was getting ready to become a mommy. I had no idea what God had in store for me. The next day would be the happiest and scariest day of my life. Since that day my life has changed so much. My whole little world shifted on its axis the day my Jack came into my life. I've never been more thankful than I am right now for the blessings of my God. Just looking at that sweet little face. Every little thing he does is magic.

This weekend we spent our first holiday with our precious boy. And what more wonderful holiday is there to celebrate with our sweet son than the resurrection of our Lord and Savior, Jesus Christ. We will spend our lives and dedicate our mission as parents to teaching our son the magnitude of what God did for us when he sent his son to die on OUR cross. We are literally eternally grateful for His sacrifice. Thank you Lord.

Jack had a great time at his first family get-togethers. He got to meet new aunts, uncles, and cousins. He got to hunt Easter eggs and even went to church for the first time with his mom and dad. Everyone was so glad to see him. It was a great weekend.

Now that Easter is over, it's time to start focusing on Jack's heart catheterization that is going to take place next Wednesday, April 18th. We got the call today with all of the information that we need and now we're in major prayer mode. We're praying for a BIG miracle that day.

Josh and I will take Jack in to be admitted into UAB at 6am. We'll get a private room where we'll then go and wait for them to get ready for him. He's the youngest, so he's the first patient of the day. They'll let me and Josh walk him to the door of the cardiac unit, then we'll give him LOTS of hugs and kisses and say one more prayer for him, then we'll have to go back to his room for the hard part. The waiting.

Jack will be put under with general anesthesia. They'll then give him an IV and then put him on the ventilator. They'll go in through his groin and up the vein. Once they're in his heart they'll just measure pressures and take some pictures. They said it could take up to four hours depending on how difficult it is to maneuver through his small veins. Once they are done, Dr. Law (the cardiologist) will call me and Josh and let us know how it went. They'll take him off the ventilator and get him breathing good on his own again and then he'll go into recovery where Josh and I will meet him. At which point I will scoop him up and love him to pieces. We'll be in recovery for around an hour and then we'll go back to his regular room for at least six hours and possibly the night.

That's the plan. We're praying that everything will go as smoothly as possible and that it will be quick and easy for him and for us. The nurse who called me today said that it will be much harder on us than it will be on him. She said the incision is tiny and shouldn't be too sore. And they're going to wait until he's under to do his IV so he won't be in pain when Mommy's not there to hold his hand.

This is his first really invasive procedure. It's his first time to be put to sleep. His first incision. His first time to be on the ventilator. His first time to be away from Mommy when they're poking at him. It's very scary for me and Josh. We just pray that God will hold him in His almighty hands. Bring him comfort if he gets scared or upset. Be with the doctors and nurses while they do their work. Let this procedure go as smoothly as possible. Allow for a quick and easy recovery. And most importantly, AMAZING results.

We are trusting our God 100% for the results that we want to hear. We know that He has an amazing plan for Jack's life and we are believing in His will. He has brought us this far and given us miracle after miracle with our sweet boy. How could we not trust Him?

"Now to him who is able to do immeasurably more than all we ask or imagine, according to his power that is at work within."

EPHESIANS 3:20

Our God is MORE than able to do MORE than we could ever ask or imagine. Miracles ARE possible.

SUNDAY, APRIL 22, 2012
Heart Cath Results

"Have I not commanded you? Be strong and courageous.
Do not be frightened, and do not be dismayed, for the Lord
your God is with you wherever you go."

JOSHUA 1:9

The days leading up to Jack's heart cath were long. I was really nervous and started breaking out in hives. I've never done that before so I decided to go to the doctor. I went to After Hours and got a couple of shots and they put me on Prednisone. It has helped me keep it under control for the past week and I am going to see my sister's allergy specialist tomorrow morning to hopefully get a more permanent solution.

The night before was tricky. We couldn't give Jack any breast milk after 3am and we had to be there at 6. I was really worried about timing it out right so that he wouldn't be starving that morning. Needless to say we got no sleep that night between trying to work out the timing and stressing over the procedure. We we're up at 2:15 giving Jack his bottle and then I was in the shower by three. We had packed enough for one night just in case we had to stay but were hoping they'd let us go. We pulled out at 4:45am and Jack watched SpongeBob on the IPAD in the car until he fell back asleep.

When we got there we were put into a regular room and

started the wait. They told us that Dr. Law would be by in a little while to talk to us before they took him back. They brought in the tiniest little hospital gown for us to put on him and let me tell you.. Nobody can make a hospital gown look cute like my boy.

Dr. Law came by around 8 and talked us through what they would do. He said they would put him under with a mask and then start his IV. He wouldn't be back there long at all before he was put under which made me feel a little bit better. I didn't want him to feel scared when we weren't back there with him. Then after they were ready he would go in through a tiny incision in his groin and then go into his heart where they would measure pressures and take pictures. He explained the risks but let us know that Jack was in a low risk category and he felt certain that it would be an easy procedure. He said he would call the phone in the room when they were done to let us know how it went. It should take him about three hours once anesthesia was done with their part.

After that Josh and I walked with the nurses down to the floor that he would be on and we walked him to the door of the OR. We kissed him a thousand times and then a few times more before I handed him to a very sweet nurse in brown scrubs. She promised to take good care of him. We watched until they rounded the corner and then I cried all the way back up to our room while people looked at me and I'm sure wondered what was wrong with the crazy sobbing lady.

When we got back we just had to settle in for a few hours of nervous waiting. I hated the thought that he was down there without me but I knew he was in good hands and was sound asleep. It was also really comforting to have a lot of family around to talk to and joke with. It made time pass really quickly. After about 3 and a half hours the phone rang.

Dr. Law told me that the procedure went well. He said Jack did fine and was resting now and we could see him soon. He said they had one episode during the procedure where his heart rate went up for about 15 minutes but then it balanced back out on its own. Other than that it all went well and there was no damage done to his veins. He told me that he had to make some rounds and would come by our room later that day to give us the details.

Then Josh and I got to go meet Jack in recovery. We practically ran. When we got there he was in his tiny little bed still hooked up to monitors. They had removed the tape from his face but the sticky residue still marked his sweet cheeks. He was still so out of it that he couldn't keep his little eyes open. He tried so hard to open them and look at us but they would just roll back into his little head. We kissed all over him and petted him while we waited for his recovery time to be over. When that time had passed we walked next to his little bed while they rolled him back to his room where our family anxiously waited for him to round the corner. They were so happy to see him and he was finally starting to come around more and open his eyes good.

When we got settled back in the nurse said I could try to feed him. Our poor baby hadn't eaten in so long. We got wrapped up in blankets and settled into a chair and he went to town on his bottle. Over half way through his 5 ounces he started throwing it all back up. It was the most he had ever thrown up at one time and it scared me and him both. We got him sat up and he got it all out and then we wrapped him in some different blankets and let him settle in for a nap in the MaMaRoo swing that they had brought in for us to use.

His little leg was still hurting from his incision plus he was really sick from the anesthesia so he didn't sleep well at all that day. He would roll around and moan like he was hurting and sick. It was so hard as a mommy to know he wasn't feeling good and I couldn't do anything about it. As far as that goes it was a really long day and an even longer night. We had to spend the night because his reaction to the anesthesia was rare for a baby and the doctors and nurses didn't really seem to know what to do for him. We just basically had to wait it out. We tried over and over to feed him, first breast milk and then Pedialyte and he just couldn't keep anything down. He eventually emptied his tummy out and started to dry heave. It was awful. We finally convinced them to start a new IV and start getting some fluids into him. We were worried and scared.

When he got his IV for the procedure they had stuck him 16 times. There were bruises and stick marks all over my poor baby's body. They had clearly had trouble finding a good vein to use with him being so little. But we didn't want that happening to him this time because he was awake and would feel everything so when it was time to stick him again you can bet Josh and I were going to be in there. They took him to a different room and three nurses worked to find a good spot. Thankfully, they got a good one on the first try in his little hand and they wrapped it well so that it wouldn't get messed up like the last one had. He had been through enough. This needed to be his last stick for the day.

When we got back to the room Dr. Law was waiting there for us. He explained exactly what he had found in the cath and the steps we would take from there.

He talked a little bit about his VSD which we already knew he had but he also told us about some narrowing at his ASD which will need to be made bigger. There is also some narrowing at his Pulmonary Valve which restricts some blood flow to his lungs. The pressures there are not dangerously elevated but are a little bit on the higher side and they will need to be mindful of that when doing his surgery. His VSD is a little bit on the small side and causes some pressure drop which again is something they needed to know about when moving forward.

Dr. Law then said that he has decided to move forward with his surgery in the next month. There is also a little bit more work in addition to the Glenn that will need to be done at the same time. One thing that will need to be done is an atrial septectomy which will make that hole (ASD) bigger. Also a Damus-Kaye-Stansel procedure which will bring the pulmonary artery over to the aorta. This allows the blood to go out both pathways so that the pressure in the ventricle is not higher than the pressure outside of it. They will also do the Glenn at the same time.

He feels that Jack has grown really well and is a nice size for this procedure and he feels that the benefits of going ahead with the procedure far outweigh the added risks. Basically, its time and we're going for it.

He said we should be made aware of a couple of things going into the surgery. Many times when they do the Glenn there will be an improvement in the saturation. But Jack's saturation is already good so there will be an improvement in his blood flow but ultimately we might not see much change in his saturations. He said they might even be lower after surgery because of all of the changes his heart will go through but there will be a nice physiological improvement for his heart for the long term. Which is really where it counts anyway.

We are still looking to do the Fontan procedure at around 2-3 years of age. So after this procedure next month his long term plan is still the same. The only changes in his overall plan are the additions he has added to the Glenn surgery. After that we'll continue on our original course of action.

He did add that Jack's heart function is really good and the valves work really well. He said that his function is fine and the problem he has is with the plumbing. He said overall he thinks everything still looks favorable and he has a really positive outlook on how everything is going to go.

From there we discussed surgeons and scheduling. He has a surgeon that he has chosen and scheduling will call us within the next couple of weeks to hammer out a specific date.

After a long night for our sweet boy, he finally started taking small amounts of breast milk the next morning and by that afternoon had successfully kept down four ounces. We finally got discharged at around 2:30 and came home. It still has taken a couple of days for him to bounce back but he thankfully woke up happy this morning and has had a great day. He has also gone back to his regular 4–5 ounces today which was a big relief for us. There is just SO much comfort in being at home with our boy. When we're at home it doesn't feel like there is anything to be afraid of.

Now we just have a month of anxious waiting ahead of us. Josh and I have decided to focus on our spiritual preparation. There is no amount of emotional or physical preparation that we can undergo that will ever render us ready to hand our son over to a surgeon in a month's time. We have decided to spend this month in the Word and in prayer because God is the only preparation that we truly need. We are praying for His hand on our sweet boy. That he will guide the hands of the surgeons, doctors, and nurses that work on Jack. That He will provide complete healing in our son and allow this surgery to be the means by which that healing comes. We know He has a purpose for this and we intend to be used to the greatest extent that we can be.

We are also praying for God's comfort and peace to be upon us during this time. As we find out more information about the surgery we grow more nervous and anxious. We are praying that God will just be with us and allow us to get through this with as much grace as possible. We know that God's plan is moving right now and we are just doing our best to have faith and trust in His plan. He is our Lord and we trust Him.

Ephesians 3:20-21 says, "Now to Him who is able to do immeasurably more than all we ask or imagine, according to his power that is at work within us, to Him be glory in the church and in Christ Jesus throughout all generations, forever and ever! Amen."

Our God is able to do immeasurably more than anything I can ask Him to do or imagine He could do for me or for Jack. He will provide healing and peace for my son and my family. I am standing on the Word of my sweet savior.

WEDNESDAY, MAY 16, 2012
Surgery Day

"But those who hope in the Lord will renew their strength.
They will soar on wings like eagles; they will run and not
grow weary, they will walk and not be faint."

ISAIAH 40:31

Well, we made it through today.

Jack is finally recovering in the CICU. Josh and I got to speak with Dr. Dabal (the surgeon) and he told us that the surgery went really well. All three procedures went great and they accomplished everything they went in to do. There were a few complications that came up during surgery, the most challenging being a heart flutter and severe bleeding. He is still bleeding now but Dr. Dabal said that it should slow down and eventually stop on its own. As far as the heart flutter goes, he had the same thing during his heart cath and so they are planning to watch his rhythms closely over the next few days and if need be they will put him on medications to balance it out. The good news is that there is no danger that he will need a pacemaker.

Right now he is sleeping and will be for most of the evening and night tonight. They were planning to try to get him off the vent tonight but then his O2 sats never rose and are sitting in the low 70s so Dr. Dabal said that he will leave him on the vent until his sats rise to the 80s and that could be Friday or Saturday. We are praying that they begin to rise soon.

Overall this was a successful day and we are on the road to recovery. We're still in a really critical place and it's still scary but we continue to trust that God is taking good care of him. We are SO thankful for all of the prayers and sweet words of encouragement that were spoken over us today. We just want to see our smiling boy again soon.

We are so thankful to our amazing God for moving this mountain today. He provided us with a miracle and we know that it's because God has big plans for our son to do something extraordinary with his life. God has shown up for us time and time again and we just hope that everyone who is following our story sees the hands of God at work in our sweet boy's little life. God is BIGGER and is able to do more than we can ask or imagine. ALL of the glory be to Him who does provide.

JEREMIAH 29:11 / ISAIAH 40:31 / EPHESIANS 3:20

SATURDAY, MAY 19, 2012

Post-Op Days One and Two

"Do not be anxious about anything, but in everything, by prayer and petition, with thanksgiving, present your requests to God. And the peace of God, which transcends all understanding, will guard your hearts and your minds in Christ Jesus."

PHILIPPIANS 4:6-7

POST-OP DAY ONE:

This was an extremely challenging day. Challenging our patience, our nerves, and our faith. Jack's saturations dropped to an extremely low point and we saw incredible, experienced doctors panic. There were moments when we were faced with the fear that our son might not make it through all of this. Seeing the faces of the doctors and hearing them make desperate phone calls was beyond scary to say the very least. It was the kind of day that no parent should ever have to live through. We are thankful now that it's over and we sincerely hope to never have another day like that one.

The comfort that we have in being believers is that God is in there with us. When it all becomes too much, He is with us. When our tears fall and our hands shake, He is with us. When we fear the unknown, He is with us. When we face our worst nightmares, He is with us. The peace that transcends all understanding settles in the room with us and we know that He is there and He is in control. His plan will always prevail and it will always be what is best. Trusting may be difficult at times when fear creeps in the back door but He is infinitely patient. Then, when we finally find it within ourselves to trust completely, God delivers on a profound and amazing promise. That if you only have faith, anything is possible. Mountains will move. Praise God for that.

Jack's saturations were lower than most babies after the BD Glenn. The doctors couldn't figure out why. By that evening, the two doctors that we are familiar and comfortable with (Dr. Law-Jack's cardiologist and Dr. Dabal- Jack's surgeon) had gone home and the doctor that was there was the CICU doctor who seemed unsure and nervous. (I want to make a note here that I feel is necessary before I go on... After spending several days in the care of this doctor, we came to know and understand his personality better. Every doctor is different. They have different personalities. Some are more positive and encouraging in their nature, others tell it like it is. We came to truly know and love this doctor and are extremely thankful for the care that he gave to Jack during his days with us.) He made many comments about how he wasn't sure what he was going to do. Needless to say it was a scary time for us. There was talk about a possible need for another surgery. They said that the times that they have had to resort to this surgery in the past, they usually had to go back in two weeks later and undo it. That would be three surgeries in a couple of weeks. They told us that they wanted to avoid that at all costs because the risks would be so much higher now that he has just come out of one surgery and would be going right back into the OR. They continued to tell us how uncommon it was for a baby to have such low sats after this surgery and how they were so unsure about what could be causing it. Also inferring that they had no idea how, or even if, they could fix it.

By that night, we had grown scared and desperate. I emailed

Dr. Dabal and told him that I wanted him to know that Jack's sats were still really low and that the doctor that was there with us was scaring us. I apologized for bothering him at home but I needed some reassurance that Jack was still going to be okay. This was the lowest, scariest moment for us yet.

Isaiah 43:2 says, "When you pass through the waters, I will be with you; and when you pass through the rivers, they will not sweep over you. When you walk through the fire, you will not be burned; the flames will not set you ablaze."

Never has this scripture been more true in my life than it was on post-op day one. We passed through the waters that day but the good news is that we were only passing through. There were moments when we may have felt like the waters were sweeping over us, like we were drowning, but we didn't drown. It is moments like these that become the defining moments of your life. You don't realize it while it's happening. You're focusing on what is happening in front of you. But God always has the bigger picture in mind. And what you discover when you look back on those moments of desperation is that through God you can find a strength inside of yourself that doesn't really belong to you. The kind of strength that you could never muster on your own. But through God, that strength is there. You may not even know it's there while it's happening. But when you look back, you can see it. Plain as day.

In Christ we are warriors. Brave, strong, tough. We are fearless.

Romans 8:31 asks us, "If God is for us, who can stand against us?" The answer is no one. No fear. No disease. No trial. Not even death.

One of my favorite songs is "Holy Wedding Day." If you're not familiar with it, I encourage you to grab a tissue, play the song and spend a minute praising Jesus for the work He did for us on that cross. Because of the cross my friends, even death has no power over us.

> *This is the story of the Son of God*
> *Hanging on a cross for me*
> *But it ends with a bride and groom*
> *and a wedding by a glassy sea*
> *Oh, death where is your sting?*
> *Cause I'll be there singing*
> *Holy, holy, holy is the Lord.*

Friends, if you are not sure if you're going to be there, I cannot express enough the urgency with which you must make that decision. As a good friend of mine recently said, every tragic day began as an ordinary day. We don't know what tomorrow holds. But with Jesus Christ as our Lord and savior, we can rest in knowing that no matter what happens in this life, there will come a day when His children will stand before Him and sing holy. My greatest prayer for every single person who is holding this book and reading these words is that you do not wait another minute. Call out to Him. He is waiting for you.

POST-OP DAY TWO:

We woke up this day determined that it was going to be a good day. We prayed for a miracle and believed that God would provide.

It was pretty early when Dr. Dabal came around the corner. I was SO happy to see him that I practically knocked people down trying to get to him. He told me that he had emailed me back but I hadn't gotten it because cell phone service at the hospital is non-existent. He instantly began to reassure me about

Jack's condition. He said that even though the saturations were still low, Jack was tolerating it well and that is what really matters. He said that they weren't happy with the sats but that they would figure out what was causing them to be so low and how to get them back up. He said that Jack was still going to be okay.

Why couldn't he have been there the night before when I was desperate for someone to say just that? Maybe God was testing my ability to rely on Him instead of the doctors for my hope and reassurance.

Message received Lord. Lesson learned.

> "Have I not commanded you? Be strong and courageous. Do not be terrified; do not be discouraged, for the Lord your God will be with you wherever you go."
>
> JOSHUA 1:9

Needless to say that post-op day two was off to a better start already. Jack's sats were still pretty low but we felt reassured that a solution was coming. Not long after Dr. Dabal left Jack's bedside the CICU doctor came by to tell us that he was going to meet with Dr. Dabal and Dr. Law and come up with a plan for Jack. They were trying to decide if taking him off the vent was a good idea. They had just ran a test on Jack with the ECHO machine where they put some saline mixed with blood which formed tiny little micro bubbles into his veins then watch where it goes. This test would tell them if any blood was passing the Glenn and going straight to the heart. This could possibly explain why his sats were so low.

Dr. Law came out of their meeting and told us that they had all agreed to leave Jack on the vent for now and to take him back for another heart cath. They felt like Jack's problem was probably one of two things. Either there was a vein that goes around the BD Glenn that used to be closed but had popped open because of the new pressure in Jack's heart. They assumed this was a possibility because of the results of the bubble test. If this was the case then that vein could be pumping blood past the Glenn and into the heart instead of taking the Glenn route to Jack's lungs. The other thing they were going to check for was just if everything from the surgery looked good. They said that because they already knew that Jack's lungs were healthy before the surgery then if everything from the surgery looked good and was working like it should, they could safely conclude that Jack's sats were just taking longer to rise to an acceptable number but that given some time, they would.

Even though we didn't want to have to do another procedure, we were relieved that they were able to promise us that some answers were coming soon. So, we signed the consent forms for the cath. The CICU doctor also told us that there was a little bit of fluid sitting between Jack's lungs and his chest and they needed to put in a chest tube to drain that fluid. So, we signed the consent forms for that too. Sure, go ahead and put three new holes in our baby, like he hasn't been through enough already... Grrr. The chest tube went in fine and instantly started to drain a pretty good amount of fluid. They said this would help the lungs to expand all the way and maybe bring his sats up a point or two. Then at 11am, they wheeled him off to the cath lab. It's funny how scared we were a few weeks ago when Jack had his first cath and now, compared to open-heart surgery, heart caths are a total walk in the park.

After waiting, and waiting, and then waiting some more, about three and a half hours to be specific, they called for me and Josh to go back. They told us that everything inside looked great. No open veins carrying blood past the Glenn. No problems with the surgery. Just a few spots on his lungs that were collapsed but that should fix itself when he started moving around, breathing hard, and coughing again. So, what they concluded was that Jack's heart function looked good and his sats will eventually rise on their own. They said that it might take some time and we should be patient but the good news is that there isn't really anything to worry about as long as his numbers stay above 60.

"Do not be anxious about anything, but in everything, by prayer and petition, with thanksgiving, present your requests to God. And the peace of God, which transcends all understanding, will guard your hearts and your minds in Christ Jesus."

PHILIPPIANS 4:6-7

SUNDAY, MAY 20, 2012

Post-Op Day Three

"Our light and momentary troubles are achieving for
us an eternal glory that far outweighs them all."

2 CORINTHIANS 4:17

This was a very eventful day for our sweet little trooper. His sats weren't great but he was hanging in there for most of the morning. They decided to go ahead and take him off the vent. We were so ready to see our boy without that breathing tube. We were excited about the possibility of him being really awake for the first time since surgery.

At 9:33am they pulled the vent tube out of his throat and he got put on heavy flow oxygen. They also pulled the NG tube out at that time. We got to see his precious little mouth for the first time in a few days. His mouth was super dry so the nurses gave us these tiny little sponge-on-a-stick things that we would dip in water and let him suck on. He liked it sometimes and got mad as fire other times. Believe me, if he didn't want it, he'd let us know.

As soon as they pulled the vent tube out he started to try to cry but his little throat was too sore to make any real noise. He could only get out faint whispery cries at first but they grew louder and stronger throughout the day. We let him suck on a passy for a while and let him chew on his favorite teething toy, Ernie G. Raff. He really went to town chewing on Ernie. He also started really opening his eyes for the first time. It was wonderful getting to see our boy again. We had missed those beautiful eyes. Later they came back and took out both of his pacing wires. Then he also got to get one drainage tube, his catheter, and his head monitor off. What a BIG day!

That evening, as Jack started to wake up more and more, he began to grow more and more fussy. He started to have little episodes where he would wake up and thrash around in his bed. He would cry his sad hoarse little cry and open his foggy eyes as much as he could. He was having headaches related to the pressure change in his head caused by the surgery. As a result of the BD Glenn, the pressure in Jack's head suddenly became the equivalent of a normal person hanging upside down for several hours. This is because his lungs are used to working really hard to pump and now they aren't having to work as hard. Now they are tensing up and pumping blood to his head. The CICU doctor said this is a normal side effect of the Glenn and would resolve itself when Jack's lungs get used to the pressure and relax. Until then he will have really bad headaches.

Although the pressure headaches are normal and expected for Glenn babies, they said that Jack seemed to react much worse than most babies. And because his sats are already low, he doesn't have much reserve for when he gets upset. Meaning, most Glenn babies whose sats are in the 80s might get upset and drop their sats to the 60s. But because Jack's sats are starting in the 60s, when he gets mad and his sats drop, it's dangerous. So, besides worrying about how much pain he was in and doing our best to console and comfort him, we were also watching the monitor and worrying about the numbers. It was a tough night for all of us.

Post-Op Day Four

"For God has not given us a spirit of fear, but of
power and of love and of a sound mind"

2 TIMOTHY 1:7

Jack was still having the pressure headaches all morning on
day four. We stayed at his bedside ready to jump up and console him every few minutes when he would stir and start to cry
and thrash around. He started having one particularly bad episode and his sats started falling into the 50s. We didn't think too
much of it because he had been doing this all night but then his
sats suddenly fell to the 40s, then the 30s, then when they hit the
20s our nurse, Ashley, yelled out for someone to get the doctor.
By the time that he got to Jack's bed, the sats had reached the
teens. If the 60s aren't good, I'm sure you can imagine how bad
the teens are.

We could see the panic in their faces as they ran around his
bed, throwing stuff and yelling out commands to each other.
Suddenly our little corner was filled with doctors and nurses.
The CICU doctor put the oxygen mask on Jack's little face and
was bagging him repeatedly trying to get his sats to rise back up
while his nurses and other doctors got stuff ready to re-intubate.
The doctor was trying to wait to see if he would snap out of it
but he never did. After a few minutes, they made a decision and

a nurse pushed the paralyzing medicine into his IV. Jack went from crying and thrashing in their arms to completely limp in one second flat. It was surreal. It was almost like we were watching a scene from a movie. But we weren't. We were there and it was our baby that was being thrown around like a ragdoll. It was our baby's monitor that was beeping and wailing. It was our baby's doctors and nurses that were yelling commands and wiping sweat off their faces. It was our baby who had crashed and it was our baby whose life they were trying desperately to save.

The CICU doctor looked back and asked if we were okay to stay and watch this. I couldn't say anything. Josh said yes. Then we watched as they pushed the tube back down his throat and got him set back up on the vent. Then the doctor bagged him some more until his sats rose back up. Then they loaded him back up on medication and got him stabilized again. What sounds like something that happened in a matter of seconds really was about 10 minutes if not longer... and certainly felt like a lifetime.

When he was done, the doctor turned to talk to me and Josh. He explained that Jack wasn't tolerating being off the vent any longer and they didn't really have a choice. They were basically just going to let him rest for a few days and give the pressure in his lungs some time to relax before they extubated him again. Really he would be better off this way because he was in so much pain when he was awake. He explained that they would likely keep him pretty heavily sedated to allow his sats to stay up and give him a few days to adjust a little more to the new pressures. In the meantime, he could sleep and wouldn't be in any pain at all.

This whole experience since Jack was born has been traumatic to say the least but if you ask me what has been the scariest moment, it was this one. It all happened so fast and was so intense that we weren't sure if Jack was going to be okay. We knew that they were re-intubating him but we didn't know exactly what was wrong or how bad it was. Or if it was going to work.

The moment was so surreal. I was frozen in fear. On the inside I had the strongest need to just go yank all of the cords off of him and just hold him in my arms. Up until this surgery, that was all he ever needed to be okay. I could pick him up and look into his big blue eyes and sing him a song and he would smile up at me as if he were saying, "Thanks Mommy, I feel better now." Standing there watching helpless as a team of doctors and nurses shove needles, tubes, and wires into his lifeless body while the monitors rage was horrifying. The worst moment of my life to date. Period.

Fear is an emotion that we can't escape. As human beings, we have been subjected to the feeling of fear since Eve took a bite of that apple. The Bible says that Adam hid from God because he was afraid. This was the first time that the Bible mentions fear. It didn't take long (The third chapter in Genesis to be exact.) for God to jump into what appears to be one of His main points throughout the entire Bible.

But the Lord God called to the man, "Where are you?" He answered, "I heard you in the garden, and I was afraid because I was naked; so I hid." Genesis 3:9-10

Fear is certainly an underlying theme throughout the Bible. God tells his people not to be afraid. He wants us to be able to lean totally upon him and not on our own understanding. It's our own understanding from which fear is born and bred. If we can master the art of truly trusting God and overcoming fear, we would find peace and rest like no promise from a doctor could ever provide.

Why is it that it's easier to find comfort in the words of a doctor than in the promises of God Himself? After all, only He really knows what's going to happen. A doctor can make me a thousand promises but he doesn't actually know what's going to happen to my son. Only God does... and He doesn't just know what's going to happen. He wrote the story of Jack's life Himself. What more comfort could I possibly need?

And yet I find myself seeking out our doctors and bombarding them with questions about Jack's condition, his prognosis, and his future. I'm constantly longing to hear them say that he'll live to be an old man with a rocking chair and a bunch of grandkids. And who's to say that heart disease will even be what ends his life? Who's to say that his life will even end? Who's to say that Jesus Christ won't come riding His white horse over the clouds tomorrow morning before all of the answers to my thousands of questions ever even mattered?

Now don't get me wrong. I'm not saying that I'm going to stop asking questions any time soon. I'm still human and no matter how much faith I am able to muster, I still have a human heart filled with fear and questions. And I also believe in medicine. I believe that God granted humans the ability to know and understand how the body works and how to fix things that are broken. Praise Him for that.

It's finding the right balance of the two that takes a real relationship with God. I believe this is what God is teaching me right now. It's a daily walk. To be able to ask our doctors all of the questions and get all of the facts and then lay it all down at the feet of the God who loves me and who most certainly loves my son... It takes a lot of faith. Sometimes I have enough. Other times I fall short. I feel like God understands. Who better understands the love of a parent for their child than our heavenly father?

I said all of that to say this... Fear is pointless. It goes against what God wants for us and from us. But knowing that doesn't make it any easier to let go of our fear and trust God. I'm working on that everyday. I haven't quite gotten it figured out yet. Probably never will. But I believe that to God, working on it is enough. That's what makes our God so amazing. He doesn't expect us to be perfect or to always get it right. He just wants our best. And right now my best is to try... and I'm trying. I really am.

With this in mind, I want to share with you some of the MANY verses in the Bible that address fear. The only way I have EVER been able to combat fear is to get into His Word. We can't change the path that we are on but we can ask Him for help. And I promise you, He will pour HIS peace that transcends all understanding into our hearts. I know because I have felt it.

"For God has not given us a spirit of fear, but of power and of love and of a sound mind."

2 TIMOTHY 1:7

"Do not fear, for I am with you; Do not anxiously look about you, for I am your God. I will strengthen you, surely I will help you, Surely I will uphold you with My righteous right hand."

ISAIAH 41:10

"Even though I walk through the valley of the shadow of death, I will fear no evil, for you are with me; your rod and your staff, they comfort me."

PSALM 23:4

"The LORD is my light and my salvation-- whom shall I fear? The LORD is the stronghold of my life-- of whom shall I be afraid?"

PSALM 21:7

TUESDAY, MAY 22, 2012

Post-Op Days Five and Six

"For you created my inmost being; you knit me together in my mother's womb. I praise you because I am fearfully and wonderfully made; your works are wonderful, I know that full well."

PSALM 139: 13-14

POST-OP DAY FIVE

This was a relatively uneventful day. Since they decided to let Jack stay on the vent for a few days, there really wasn't much going on. Dr. Dabal came by and talked to me. He told me that Jack does have an infection but they weren't sure where it was. He said that infections are really common and they would just treat it and then try to extubate again. He told me that when babies are on so many pain medications, they become addicted very easily. So, they were going to start him on Ativan and Methadone to help wean him off of the Morphine and other medications he has been on. He said that it was something they pretty much always have to do and really wasn't a big deal. Jack pretty much just slept all day and rested.

POST-OP DAY SIX

Jack's temperature started to go up this morning and it scared me, of course. When the doctors came by doing rounds they told us that he had an infection in his airway caused by bacteria in his vent tube. He said it was a common kind of infection and was very treatable. It's called Tracheitis. He is getting two IV antibiotics and one inhaled antibiotic. Our nurse explained to us that he should react well to the antibiotics since he has never had any before. God willing, those antibiotics will knock the infection out completely in the next couple of days and we won't have to worry about that anymore. They did run a test this evening on his inflammation and it came back significantly less than it has been which was a really good sign that the antibiotics are working.

The main problem right now with the infection is that they can't extubate him again until the infection is gone. The plan to extubate went from possibly Wednesday to hopefully Thursday or Friday. We are nothing if not patient so we don't mind the wait. We just want our boy better, doesn't matter how long it takes.

In other news, Jack had two really big poops today. I know you probably don't care about my son's poop but he has been having trouble going so it was a big deal to us. Way to go Baby Jack!

We should get the results of the cultures they drew tomorrow afternoon and hopefully they'll be better than they have been, meaning his infection is dying. His sats are still sitting mostly in the 60s but are slowly improving. They're giving him Tylenol to treat his fever but hopefully that will start to go down too and we can drop the Tylenol. He's getting a PICC line right this minute. By the time we're allowed back in at 8:30 they should be done with that and that will lower his risk of infection related to his central line which they are taking out as soon as they get his PICC line in.

We're making progress slowly but surely. Today Dr. Dabal told Josh that he doesn't consider Jack a sick baby. That was reassuring to hear. This situation is such a roller coaster and there are ups and downs every single day. This morning I was bawling my eyes out, terrified. This evening I was laughing my head off, comforted. You never know what they day will bring. My faith in God is the only thing that brings any sort of stability right now. I truly don't know how people go through things like this without God in their corner. For me, I just constantly remind myself that we are going through this for a reason... BUT we're only going through. It will all be over pretty soon and we'll look back and be able to see the evidence of God being with us through this whole experience.

I believe in my heart that God does have a plan for Jack far beyond this moment in his life. I believe that God has a plan for Jack as an adult. I always have. Sometimes when fear creeps in it becomes harder to see the bigger picture. It becomes hard to see past this moment. However, I know that God ALWAYS sees the bigger picture. He wrote it. He knows exactly what day Jack will take his first step. He knows that Jack's first word will undoubtedly be "Momma." He knows who Jack will marry. He knows how many souls will spend eternity in heaven as a result of the impact that my sweet Jack had on the world.

My comfort is in knowing that Jack is having and will continue to have an impact on this world. God sometimes allows us to go through trials to teach us lessons and also to use us. I believe that we are most certainly learning lessons right now. We're learning about having faith, about how to trust God completely, about how to be patient, about how sometimes God's plan works out so much better than you could have imagined when you just trust Him and allow Him to do things in His own timing. Sometimes we look back and think, thank goodness that God didn't give us what we were asking for. He most certainly always knows best.

"And therefore the Lord waits to be gracious to you; and therefore He lifts Himself up, that He may have mercy on you and show loving-kindness to you. For the Lord is a God of justice. Blessed are all those who wait for Him, who expect and look and long for Him."

ISAIAH 30:18

"For you created my inmost being; you knit me together in my mother's womb. I praise you because I am fearfully and wonderfully made; your works are wonderful, I know that full well."

PSALM 139: 13-14

FRIDAY, MAY 25, 2012

Post-Op Day Seven and Eight: Bitterness and God's Promises

"You need to persevere so that when you have done the will of God, you will receive what He has promised."

HEBREWS 10:36

POST-OP DAY SEVEN

Jack had a really good day. His temp jumped around but the doctor said that he didn't want to worry about a low grade fever because that just meant that Jack's body was really fighting the infection. His sats were pretty average. Not great, but not bad.

But the biggest event of yesterday was that Jack opened his eyes for the first time in over a week. --Well, he technically opened his eyes on Saturday when he was extubated but they were foggy and he couldn't seem to focus on anyone. That day it was more scary than happy.-- But this time it was wonderful. His eyes were clear and beautiful. They were Jack's eyes. He opened them and looked right at me and I melted. I love that boy so much. He's my whole world.

POST-OP DAY EIGHT

Yep. We're still here. Jack had a really good night with his favorite night nurse, Katie. The only little incident in the night was that he started throwing up stomach acid around 8:30 but she quickly put in a second NG tube to catch it since he has the vent tube down his throat and can't really throw up. She caught a lot of the acid at first so they decided to leave the tube in so it wouldn't collect in his tummy. Now it's draining through his NG tube but there hasn't been nearly as much since last night.

This morning we were really hoping for extubation, however his sats were lower and temp was higher this morning than it had been all night. When the doctors made rounds they said that the top section of Jack's right lung has collapsed because of all of the fluid from the tracheitis. Now they are thinking he probably has pneumonia. They are still treating him with the two IV antibiotics and one inhaled antibiotic and they decided that they would just change the vent settings for the day and see if they could get his lung to open back up. If they can't do that by tomorrow morning, they will have a specialist come and give Jack a treatment where they will put a little probe with a video camera down into his lungs and look around then it will spray saline into his lungs and suction out all of the junk. When the doctors came by this evening they seemed to think that his 4:00 x-ray showed improvement in his lung so hopefully by morning it will be better.

In situations like these, I have found that it is easy to become bitter. It wears on you over time and you start to feel your attitude change. When Jack was born and they told us that he had a heart condition, bitterness was inescapable. I had to work to rid myself of that emotion and it took time and some serious soul searching to come to terms with our new way of life and uncertain future.

When I went into the hospital in January to give birth to my son, I assumed that it would go exactly as I had pictured it a million times. I never dreamed that it would turn out the way it did.

When Josh told me that there was something wrong with Jack's heart, my first reaction was fear and second was bitterness. Why Jack? Why us? Why me? Why not the lady who smoked when she was pregnant? Or the woman who talked about how there's nothing wrong with a drink or two? Why do those people get healthy babies and my baby is the one who is sick?

I had to go through a grieving period of sorts. I experienced the seven stages of grief. First there was shock and denial. (How is this possible? Is this a dream? This can't be happening to us.) Then pain and guilt. (Was it something I did? Is it my fault he's sick?) Next was anger and bargaining. (I'll do anything if you'll just make him better, God.) Then depression, reflection, and loneliness. (I'm scared of what will happen. I cry all the time.) Then there was the upward turn. (Maybe it's not so bad. If he has to be sick, at least it's this and not that. Things could always be worse.) Next was reconstruction and working through. (I don't like this but I can't change it so I'll just face it.) Then lastly I reached acceptance and hope. (Jack is going to be okay. We will trust God and watch Him work a miracle. Despite the situation, I'm thankful that He has chosen to use us.)

As I have come to terms with my son's condition and accepted what our life as a family and Jack's life will be like, I have realized that I would never be strong enough to handle this hand we've been dealt without the love and peace of God in my life. On the days when I start to try to take control of everything, including myself and my emotions, away from God and into my own hands, I sink quickly. Yesterday was one of those days.

After 11 days in the hospital... 11 days of not holding my son... 11 days of watching him hurt... 11 days of being constantly terrified... 11 days of watching monitors... 11 days of listening to doctors... 11 days of tears... I got mad.

When they made me leave the CICU at 6:30am for shift

change, everything looked good. Jack had a good night and was sleeping like a lamb. His sats were up and temp was down. We were thinking that when we went back at 8:30 we would be ready for extubation. However, when we did go back in, things were not how we had left them. His sats were back down and temp was back up. The doctor told us that part of his right lung had collapsed and he had a touch of pneumonia.

I was like, "You're kidding, right?" I mean, just when we thought we were on the right track, more bad news? Grrrr... . Right from the beginning of the day I allowed my attitude to plummet. I let anger and frustration rush in and take over. I was suddenly mad at everything and everyone. Baby Jack's soft spoken, ordinarily overly optimistic mom was on hiatus. I had let the bitterness come in and take over.

I won't go into details about everyone who made me mad... We'll just say it was a rough day. I can only imagine what everyone was saying when I wasn't around. "Stay out of Crystal's way. She is in a foul mood." I was just so tired of seeing my baby in that bed. I was tired of watching them stick needles into his skin like it didn't hurt. I was tired of watching the monitors get better, then worse. I was tired of hearing the doctors say maybe tomorrow. I was tired of the new nurse telling me stuff I already knew. Mostly I was just tired, physically, mentally, spiritually and emotionally.

Bitterness creeps in like a thief in the night, robbing us of our peace. Even in the midst of the biggest storm of our lives, we can have peace. Ultimately it's up to us. We can choose bitterness or we can choose peace. As a result of my day of bitterness I ended the evening feeling guilty, heavy-hearted, and nauseated. And as a result of my bad mood, pretty much everyone else was in a bad mood too. I noticed that everyone else was talking about what a terrible day it was. What an awful nurse we had. What bad news we had received. I realized that as the mom, I set the tone of the day for everyone. I can take yucky news and make it sound like a pretty good report. Or I can take decent news and make it sound like the worst report ever. I guess since I'm the mom, I get to decide... indirectly, of course. I suppose that nobody wants to be happy if I'm sad and nobody wants to be sad if I'm happy.

Natalie Grant describes the battle with bitterness well in her song "*Held.*"

> *This hand is bitterness*
> *We want to taste it, let the hatred know our sorrow*
> *The wise hand opens slowly to lilies of the valley*
> *and tomorrow*
> *This is what it means to be held,*
> *how it feels when the sacred is torn from your life*
> *and you survive*
> *This is what it is to be loved and to know*
> *that the promise was*
> *when everything fell, we'd be held*

I like the part where she says we want to let the hatred know our sorrow. Sometimes when we grieve, we just have to get mad. It's part of the process. Even though I've been through the grieving process, I am revisiting some of those steps right now. Bitterness is a tough one. It's easy to fall into and hard to pull ourselves back out of. Anger is easy. Why not? Why not blame anyone and everyone else? Why not yell, scream and punch walls. Why not?

I don't think God gets mad at us for getting angry. I think that He wants us to trust Him and believe in His plan. I think that the more disciplined I become, the less bitter I will be. God's word is full of precious promises that remind us that there is no reason to be bitter. He has a reason why He allows us to go through certain things. He has a plan to get us through. So, when things seem really bad and our mountains seem really tall, we can rest assured that it only means that God thinks we're strong enough to face it and brave enough to be tested and used.

I find myself being constantly reminded that God's ultimate plan for us goes beyond this life we are in. He sees us from an eternal perspective. And just like we allow our children to learn difficult lessons when they're young because we know it will help them become stronger, more successful adults, God views us the same way. Sometimes we have to go through difficult things in this lifetime that don't make sense to us. But He always has a plan and sometimes the things we are going through now have eternal implications. Deep, serious, soul-changing, eternal implications. It's difficult for us to understand in the moment. And it's painful. And that's hard. But we have to remember that He is there. And when His plans don't make sense and we feel scared, alone, hurt and bitter, those are the times when we need to just be held. And when we choose to lay it down, He will pour peace into us that will settle our souls and dissolve all of the anger and fear that we've been holding onto.

Post-Op Day Fourteen: Catching Up

"And we know that in all things God works for the good of those who love him, who have been called according to his purpose."

ROMANS 8:28

Two weeks ago today my son had open-heart surgery. Even now, after sitting in a hospital for two straight weeks, it's hard to believe. I think sometimes that I'll wake up and this will all have been a dream and that Jack will get to be a regular kid. That one day I will be able to watch him run and play in the yard without making him take breaks and watching to see if he's turning blue. That a cold won't be the scariest thing in the world. That a cold will just be a cold.

But as far as I can tell, I'm not dreaming. But the good news is that God is in control of our little world. And I'm quite certain that He has a BIG plan for my son. If my sweet boy has to be sick and has to go through all of this then at least we can rest in the promise that our God is sovereign. He rules over all people and all things and is in absolute control.

...And who wants to be normal anyway? Normal is totally overrated.

I haven't written things down much this past week. I have just been staying with Jack as much as I could since he's been awake a lot more and so I haven't had much extra time. I will do my best now to get you guys up to date on what's been going on around here.

First of all, we're still in the CICU and probably will be for at least a few more days. We've hit a few more bumps along the way but overall he is doing better and it seems like we are finally headed in a good direction. He has a killer team of doctors and nurses who are working diligently to fix him. Last night when we walked back in after shift change, there was a "class" going on where one of his doctors was brainstorming with the team about how to get Jack's sats up.

In my last entry, we were on day eight and Jack was battling an infection. His lungs were junky and they weren't able to extubate as soon as we had hoped. Jack was put on several antibiotics and since then that infection has completely cleared. They tried for a PICC line in his arm but it failed. A couple of days later they tried again in the other arm and failed again. At this point our poor baby looks a lot like a used pin cushion. Thankfully he was knocked out both times and didn't feel the pokes. He does have bruises but they are healing now. The day after the second try for the PICC, the doctor decided to just go for another central line and take out the old one. The point of all of this was that his original central line had been in way too long and was in danger of causing an infection but they needed a good line that they could use to draw blood gasses and give his meds. They finally got the new CL and took out the old one. But before they took the old one out they sent off blood cultures from that line. Those cultures came back positive for an infection in the blood which was terrifying because when the doctors talked to us about infections they always said that the only infections that scare them are blood infections. They assumed that the blood culture was contaminated because of the line being so old but they couldn't be sure for a couple of days. So, we had to live with that added fear for a few days but it turned out that there was not really any infection in the blood, or anywhere else for that matter.

His lungs finally started to look clearer and his sats were hanging out in the 50s and 60s but then they discovered a new infection this past weekend, similar to the original one we had just gotten over. Plus he had spiked a fever that we couldn't seem to shake. So, extubation was put off a few more days. BUT, finally on Sunday morning, after nearly two long weeks, it was time. They pulled the tube out and turned the vent off. It was a BIG day. Jack fussed all day because he didn't like the new nasal cannula that they put in his nose and the tube that was still going down his nose into his belly. He tried to pull those out every chance he got which meant me and Josh spent most of the day trying to keep his hands away from his face. He also still didn't feel great because of his fever and so he threw a few little fits. We watch the sat monitor all day praying it would be different this time and he wouldn't have those scary dips in the numbers when he got upset like he did last time he was extubated. It was a long, intense day but this time it was better.

Over the last few days Jack has kept a fever. He has been tested for every infection and virus that can be tested for and all have come back negative. The doctors seem to think he has some kind of respiratory virus that is keeping his temperature up and his lungs junky. He is coughing hard and throwing up a lot of thick mucus. He will start coughing and then gag and then throw up. The fever is really high and persistent.

We are also dealing with withdrawals from all of his pain

meds. Our doctor explained to us that 100% of babies who are on the pain meds after surgery become addicted and then withdraw when they are coming off of them. He is now off of the two pain meds he was on and is now on Methadone and Ativan to help ease the transition. The withdrawals have been hard to watch because he shakes and seems really miserable. This morning the doctor decided that the withdrawals were too intense and she decided to go back up on the Methadone and wean him a little bit slower. Hopefully we'll be fully done with the pain meds in a day or two. What's really crazy about all of this is that before surgery, I was reluctant to even give Jack any Tylenol.

Just a couple of days ago we started having another problem. He was having a strange side effect to one of the drugs that he really needs. He is on a drug called Sildenafil which is actually Viagra. It dilates the blood vessels in his lungs which helps his heart work more efficiently. Jack really needs this medicine to help with his saturations but this weekend the nurses started to notice that his little "man part" was always standing up when they changed his diapers. They told the doctors about it and they told the nurses to watch it for a while. After several hours of this, they realized that something was wrong. They called the urologists who then came down to take a look. They told us that if it continued to be erect for more than four hours at a time it could possibly cause permanent impotence. The only way to solve this problem was to give him a shot right through his little man part. Funnily enough, when Josh was signing the consent form for them to give him the shot, he just happened to glance in Jack's diaper to check one last time and guess what? It was down. I guess Jack heard what was coming and was not about to let that happen.

--------- So, where do we stand right now?

Jack still has the massive fever that we can't seem to break just yet. He is getting fed through an NG tube that goes into his tummy and is tolerating feeds well but won't be able to try a bottle until after his fever breaks and they test him to make sure he can swallow good. He is finally awake and alert for most of the day and his eyes are clear, blue, and beautiful. He is watching Spongebob on the Ipad which we have rigged up to hang from some medical equipment over the side of his bed. He is also playing with toys and being held for most of the day just like he would be at home. No smiles yet but I am determined to get the first smile although Dr. Alten (Our CICU doctor for the week) is in a contest with me for that. All of his surgical wounds are pretty much healed and his scar looks great. Tomorrow we even get to start putting onesies on him.

Our goal is to break the fever and get him past this virus. Continue to wean him off the meds and Nitric and then eventually wean him down on the oxygen and get rid of the high flow nasal cannula. It's pretty likely that we'll go home on oxygen but we can certainly handle that and it should only be for a couple of months.

Jack has been on SO many meds and antibiotics that it will be imperative when we get home that we keep him as healthy as possible. If he were to get sick it would be so much more difficult to get him over it because he has had such heavy doses of so many different antibiotics (at one point he was on 13 different antibiotics at one time!) Not to mention his heart issues and recent surgery. We will really have to enforce the "no kids" rule for a while and probably keep him at home for a good while. Believe me, nobody hates that more than I do because I LOVE to get my sweet boy out and show him off BUT I will make any and every sacrifice to keep my boy healthy.

----------- You're talking about when you come home... but are y'all ever coming home?

Yes! We will be getting out of here eventually. When? We don't know. Right now we have to focus on the fever. Then he has to get off the meds and Nitric. Then we have to wean down the oxygen. Then we have to make sure his sats are living in the high 70s to low 80s consistently. Then we can go out to the floor. Then we can focus on learning to take bottles regularly again. Then once all of that has been accomplished we can talk about going home. Once we get home a home health nurse will be assigned to us who will come and set up our oxygen system and teach us how to use it. She will come every so often to make sure we have what we need and are doing okay. Then we'll start our frequent visits to clinic to make sure everything with his heart is working right.

Now is definitely not the best time to ask me about the Fontan. After this crazy ordeal, I am currently refusing to come back. Me and Jack are formulating a plan to run away to Mexico to live on the white sandy beaches. NO MORE SURGERY for my boy. Maybe by the time he's two and a half years old I will reconsider. Maybe.

"For dominion belongs to the Lord and he rules over the nations."

PSALMS 22:28

"And we know that in all things God works for the good of those who love him, who have been called according to his purpose."

ROMANS 8:28

"As the heavens are higher than the earth, so are my ways higher than your way and my thoughts than your thoughts."

ISAIAH 55:9

Post-Op Day
Seventeen and Eighteen

"Now faith is confidence in what we hope for and assurance about what we do not see. This is what the ancients were commended for."

HEBREWS 11: 1-2

POST-OP DAY 17

These past couple of days have pretty much been dedicated to accomplishing the following things.

1. Maintain good sats (between 75-85)
2. Wean oxygen
3. Stop throwing up/diarrhea
4. Get fever down
5. Start eating
And an added bonus of sprouting new teeth!

The mysterious fever has been really throwing everyone for a loop. Jack has been tested for every single possible cause and all tests are negative. The good news is that he doesn't have any infections or other scary issues like that. The bad news is that if we can't figure out where the fever is coming from, we can't figure out how to make it go away. Hence, the waiting game.

In the meantime, we have been battling some throwing up

and diarrhea. It started a couple of days ago. It's really traumatic because when he starts throwing up he'll cough and gag and dry heave for a few minutes. He literally gags so hard he stops breathing and his little face turns purple. We have to pat his back really hard to help him. Because he is on the TP tube which delivers the breast milk directly into his small intestine, he has no food in his belly to throw up. He's throwing up stomach acid which is brown and gross. Then two nights ago he threw up blood. The doctor thinks it was possibly caused by a tear in the lining of his stomach or throat because of all of the trauma to them over the past few weeks with all of the tubes going in and out combined with the constant throwing up. It was really a terrifying moment but it only happened that one time and I pray it never happens again.

The diarrhea has been rough because he has the world's worst case of diaper rash and his little bottom just hurts. We have about four different creams that we are putting on him every time we change him and hopefully it will start to get better now that the diarrhea has pretty much stopped. It's also rough because every time he poops they have to change his central line dressing because it gets nasty germs on it and that could cause an infection. The skin under the dressing is incredibly raw because they keep having to tear tape off of it and put new tape on. He's all broken out and his skin is bright red and so sore but they can't treat it because they have to be able to stick tape to his skin to cover the central line.

His sats have finally started to improve and he is doing really well now off the vent. When he's on 100% high flow oxygen he is satting in the 80s like a rock star. They need to wean him down and then eventually switch him to low-flow before we can go out to the floor so they've been working on that for the past few days. Yesterday they decided to just give it a try. They just went from five liters of high flow to two liters of low-flow. Jack didn't respond too well and after a few hours of low sats, they had to put him back on high flow. The main problem with that process yesterday was that his little face is as broken out and chapped as his bottom. They keep having to take that tape off of his face and put new tape on every time they adjust his oxygen because he has to get a different nasal cannula for each type of flow. Yesterday it was really bad. His face is broken out and red and raw. He would scream and cry when they touched it. They kept changing the tape and it was just heartbreaking when they would pull the tape off. It hurt him so bad. Yet again, though, nothing can be done to treat the skin because they have to be able to stick that tape to his skin.

Jack hasn't had a bottle since the night before surgery which was almost three weeks ago now. For babies it's dangerous to let them go this long without drinking from a bottle because they lose their ability to suck and swallow. But, because he was on the vent for so long and then his tummy has been sick since he came off the vent, he hasn't been able to try a bottle yet. Today we tried a bottle and he gagged and started dry heaving before he even took the first swallow. We decided not to try again today because it's so hard to see him sick like that. We'll try again tomorrow. We also met with someone from speech that talked to us about the therapy that they will do to re-teach Jack how to take a bottle if need be. She also told us about several tests they will do before he can really start drinking anyway. They have to make sure that his vocal cords weren't damaged during surgery and that they can completely close when he swallows so that he doesn't aspirate.

On top of all of the other battles that our sweet boy has been fighting, he actually got his first tooth today. We had noticed that he was really fussy and extra slobbery for the past couple of days but he has been teething for a while now so we didn't think too much of it. People have told us that it usually takes a few months from the time they start teething until they actually get their first tooth. The nurse ordered some orajel from the pharmacy after she noticed how much he was chewing on things. Then when she put the oragel on his gums she felt his little tooth. Josh and I laugh because we never even gave him orajel at home and this evening our doctor came by and told the nurse to give him a dose of Morphine to help with his teething pain. He may be the only baby in the history of the world to get Morphine for teething.

It has been a challenging couple of days but we see small improvements in him each day. Right now we are just happy to see his eyes open and clear and to catch a few tiny smiles here and there. It's a joy to us just to reach the point of him getting his first tooth. There have definitely been those terrifying moments when we weren't sure if we would make it here. What is just a tooth to most people is a BIG moment for us. Our son is alive and getting better each day. He's a real miracle. At this point we feel like we can see the light at the end of the tunnel and we are satisfied with where we are in the journey because as much as we'd love to be home, we're just glad that we aren't in a place of fearing for his life. This place seems safer. Seems closer to home.

POST-OP DAY 18

What a difference a day makes!

Today has been a big day for our boy!

1. First of all, his temp has officially migrated down to the low-grade range and stayed there for 24 hours. It's not perfect but much better.

2. We're weaning off of most of the pain meds and some of the antibiotics.

3. His diaper rash is way better today. He still screams when its diaper changing time but his bottom looks so much better.

4. Most of his diarrhea is gone and throwing up has stopped completely.

5. His central line area is looking better because it hasn't had to be changed as much today.

Now for the BIG things that happened today...

First thing this morning Jack's oxygen got changed over to low-flow and he is holding strong! Sats in the 70s and 80s all day... even when he's mad! Way to go Baby Jack! Dr. Dabal came by and said that if he keeps this up for a few days, we might not have to go home on oxygen!!

Then after lunch we got to take our little man on a wagon ride around the hospital. We loaded up all of his portable equipment and pulled him around for about 15 minutes. He liked it until the end and then he got mad and demanded to be put back into his bed.

Then he took a one ounce bottle of breast milk by mouth and didn't throw up at all. Then later he took a two ounce bottle. This was a HUGE step for him. No therapy. No G-tube surgery. Praise God.

Dr. Dabal told us that at this rate we could be on the floor by Tuesday and home in a week. Today has been the best day. We couldn't be happier with the progress! God is good.

"Now faith is confidence in what we hope for and assurance about what we do not see. This is what the ancients were commended for."

HEBREWS 11:1-2

WEDNESDAY, JUNE 6, 2012

Post-Op Day 21: Three Weeks Later

"Give thanks to the Lord, for He is good;
His love endures forever."

PSALM 107:1

POST-OP DAY TWENTY-ONE

Well the biggest thing that has happened around here lately is that we FINALLY got moved to our very own room out on the floor. (For those of you wondering… When I say "floor" I am talking about the Pediatric Cardiology Unit which is where pediatric heart patients go after their stay in the CICU.) We were originally told that we would spend two nights in CICU and two to three nights on the floor. So far we have spent a total of twenty nights in the CICU and we're working on night two on the floor. We've been told that we could make it home by this weekend but it will depend on how Jack does over the next few days with a few different things.

Overall Jack's health has improved greatly in the past week. He is completely infection and virus free right now and his fever has been gone for two whole days. His white blood cell count is down to the lowest it's been since before surgery and his inflammation number is zero.

The main focus though has always been on Jack's saturations.

His saturations have been doing okay since he was extubated the second time. Most kids in Jack's position generally sat in the 80s after surgery. Jack gave the doctors a good scare when he started satting in the 50s and 60s but they realized pretty quickly that Jack tolerates lower saturations and doesn't get too blue like other kids would. They still have high hopes that his sats will rise with time but they don't know how long it will take. The first time he was extubated his sats were really low and he ended up having to be reintubated in an emergent situation when his sats dropped into the teens. Thankfully, that hasn't happened this time. He isn't having the pressure issues he was having the first time that contributed to his low saturations but also just having some extra time helped give his saturations a chance to slowly rise to a more stable area. This past week when he was still on high-flow oxygen his saturations were really great. They were in the high 70s and low 80s all the time. They changed him over to low-flow two days ago and his sats dropped back down into the high 60s and low 70s, which is not great but is still okay for Jack. Right now he is still on low-flow oxygen at three liters and 100%. We are likely going to have to go home on oxygen unless they can wean it and keep his saturations the same. We will see what happens over the next few days as they start the weaning process.

Other than weaning his oxygen, Jack also has to prove that he can get back into a regular routine with his milk and that has been more of an issue for us than we expected. Jack has always been a great eater and has gained weight well. But, after surgery he didn't have any milk for five days and then started tube feeding. He was on the vent for so long that his little tummy got used to the tube feeding that went past his belly and he isn't used to having food in his tummy. Now we are trying to feed him and he is having a lot of trouble. When he does eat well, he usually throws it back up. But mostly it's just that he won't eat to begin with. He chews on his bottle and will sip a little bit but won't really get into it like he normally would. He did have a good day with eating yesterday and we thought we were past the rough spot so they pulled his tube out but after a long day of not eating hardly at all today, they had to put the tube back in and start him on tube feeds again. Even though this is a step back, it is important to know that he's getting the nutrition he needs right now. We will continue to try to bottle feed every few hours and see if he will take it. Hopefully over the next day or so he will pick back up with eating and we can pull the tube back out.

We have also had some issues with withdrawals again today. The new CICU doctor for this week sent us out to the floor with the plan to go back up on his withdrawal meds (Methadone and Ativan) because he believes that the fevers and other mysterious symptoms that Jack has had for the past week were from withdrawals. Then the nurse practitioner that was seeing us on the floor changed it back to the weaning doses because Jack seemed to be doing so well yesterday and last night. Today, however, has been a rough day for our little man. He has just been super fussy all day and crying like he was sick or like something was hurting him. We held and rocked him all day but nothing really seemed to soothe him. So, the nurse practitioner decided to give him an amped up dose of Ativan to check for withdrawals and he instantly changed. So... withdrawals it is. Now we are going back up a tiny bit on Ativan and just staying the same on the Methadone for tonight. They will continue to try to wean him off of them but they believe it's more important that withdrawals don't interfere with his recovery than for him to try to hurry off of the drugs. They have promised us that he will be off of both of them just fine within a few days.

Lastly, as if our poor sweet boy hasn't been through enough

already… He got his SECOND tooth today. On top of everything else, Jack has gotten his first two teeth while he has been in the hospital. He's getting orajel and chewing a lot but other than that, he's just extra fussy and doesn't feel good. Hopefully the pain and irritation from that will subside by tomorrow.

I know it still sounds like a lot, but compared to where we were just a week or two ago, it's nothing. We know that everything I just mentioned will get better with time. Most of it, in just a few more days. The most important thing right now is that we are finally seeing BIG sweet smiles from our baby boy everyday. He feels like playing more now and wants to be held. He's watching lots of Spongebob and just all around seeming more like himself. We are also SO relieved to be here in the room with him. Having our own space is great but the best thing about getting our own room is that he is all ours now. The nurses and doctors come in to check on him often but in between, it's just the three of us. We're changing diapers, rocking, playing and cuddling just like we would if we were at home. AND we're here with him all night. Even when he's awake at three in the morning refusing to take a bottle or go back to sleep, we're just thankful to be with him and see his sweet face. God is good my dear friends. He is good to us. He has answered our prayers and I have no doubt that He will continue to do so and we will see great things from this boy in his lifetime.

Welcome Home
Baby Jack

"For I know the plans I have for you," declares the Lord. "Plans to prosper you and not harm you. Plans to give you hope and a future."

JEREMIAH 29:11

After twenty-four long days and nights in the hospital, we finally got the news we'd been waiting for. On Thursday, our nurse practitioner told us that if everything went well over night, we could probably go home in the morning.

After we figured out that Jack was still withdrawing and that was why he seemed to feel so bad all the time, they went back up on his Ativan and kept his Methadone the same. They decided that it would be best to wean him slower, even if that meant sending him home on both drugs. We asked a lot of questions about each of the meds and their effect on him, especially long term, and they explained everything to us and made us feel better about it. He has been on a tiny dose of each drug since we left the hospital and has been weaning slowly. Both of these drugs, especially the Ativan just make Jack super chill and not really himself. We didn't really like that he was on either drug but it was certainly better than seeing him as sick and miserable as he was when he was withdrawing. The pharmacy at the hospital set up the prescriptions for us so that each syringe was already filled with the correct dosage so that there wouldn't be any risk of us giving him too much. As the week went by, he went from .3 to .2 to .1, so each different dosage was in a different plastic baggy that was appropriately labeled and our nurse practitioner made a calendar so that we would know exactly when to give what dosage. Those who know me best know how much I can truly appreciate that kind of organization. He is now completely off of both of the drugs. He was still withdrawing all the way up until a couple of days ago but it seems like that is almost completely over with now. Thank goodness.

They also sent us home on four other medications. He is on one for his tummy, one for his high blood pressure, one for his fluid output, and one for the pressure in his lungs. All six of these medications, some of them being given two or three times throughout the day, leave us with 15 different dosages of medication throughout each day. Six of them are given at one time in the morning when Jack first wakes up. They're all oral and he HATES them all. It is a serious battle to get all of these meds into him every single time. Sometimes he screams, kicks, and spits it all back out. Other times he is a real trooper. We've tried mixing them with milk.. which he then refuses to drink. We've tried pretty much any trick you can think of and nothing really works. It will be a battle until they tell us we can stop giving the meds. We really hate having to give him the meds because of how upset he gets but we just remind ourselves that he needs it and it won't be forever.

They also sent us home on oxygen. They told us that we would have one unit for when we were at home and then something portable for when we go to our doctor appointments and clinic visits. So, Friday morning before we were discharged from the hospital the guy from the med supply company came in hauling this massive amount of equipment that was all for us.

He had to teach us how to use everything and it was a big lesson. Not too complicated but there are a lot of parts and a lot to remember. It consists of one massive home unit that will sit in a general location with 50 feet of tubing that could pretty much reach anywhere in our house. Then we have four large sized tanks for when we're out of the house. Jack is really great about the nasal cannula being on his face. We use medical tape to keep it on his face and try to only change it every few days because he hates to have the tape pulled off. Most of the time he doesn't notice it. Every now and then we will look over at him and he will have pulled it down into his mouth. Silly boy.

Last Tuesday we had Jack's post-op visit with his pediatrician, Dr. Farr. Going out with the portable oxygen tank wasn't too bad. It's on wheels and is kind of hard to steer, especially combined with the stroller. It definitely takes a team. Luckily, my mom and aunt both got to go with me so I had plenty of help. Dr. Farr said that Jack's lungs sounded great which was the main concern after all of the issues we had post-op. He said that everything looked great and the only concern he had was Jack's weight. When we were admitted to the hospital Jack weighed 15 pounds and 7 ounces. When they weighed him on Tuesday he only weighed 14 pounds and 13 ounces. That was exactly what he had weighed 5 weeks earlier at his 4 month check-up. Dr. Farr said that it is imperative that Jack continue to gain weight steadily as he had up until surgery and stay in the average to above average range. He said that weight loss was to be expected after such a rocky hospital stay but that now we have to try to bump him back up to a good weight for his age pretty quickly. So he told me to start adding a teaspoon and a half of calorie adding formula to his milk. When we were in the hospital the lactation specialist spun my milk and figured out that it has 25 calories which is more than formula so that was good news but he hasn't been able to get back to the amount of ounces he was taking before surgery yet which has contributed to the weight loss. Before surgery he was taking 6 ounces every 3–5 hours. After surgery he didn't take any milk at all for 5 days, then he was started back up really slowly and he eventually got to 35CCs an hour which is what he got for the remainder of his stay excluding the time period where we tried to bottle feed him and he threw it all up. The 35CCS an hour was going in through his TP tube and that allowed him to receive a steady amount of nutrition. But, before we could leave the hospital he had to start drinking from his bottle again. We started slowly and reached 2 ounces every 3–5 hours before we left. Now, two weeks later, we are back up to around 5 ounces. He's doing good moving up. It just takes time for his little tummy to readjust after all the trauma it's been through.

Other than all of those big things, Jack is doing great at home and is flourishing in his regular environment. He has been struggling with his sleeping because of the withdrawals but is finally starting to sleep a little better. He is playing and laughing all the time and is really getting his little personality back. His days consist of watching cartoons and cuddling with Mommy, playing, eating, napping, and then playing with his Daddy when he gets home from work. His nights consist of a mixture of sleeping and keeping Mommy up… but he's totally worth it.

I can't even begin to express how much God has blessed us throughout this experience. It's not at all what we asked for….but we've learned SO much along the way. We are SO thankful to be home and to begin the process of putting this experience behind us and settling back into our normal lives with our sweet boy. His life is even more precious to us now that we have faced the fear of the unknown. We truly see our five month old son as a warrior and he is braver than either of us could ever dream of being. I know in my heart that God allowed this to happen for a very specific reason. Though I can't see it now, I know that someday when I am looking at my son as a grown-up who is an extraordinary man of God, I'll be able to see exactly what God was doing when we were walking through this storm. I believe that whatever God's plan is for Jack, it's something big and that he will walk through this life with more purpose than most people do.

Most people say that they can't imagine what we have been through this past month. That's true. I couldn't have imagined it even a short month ago. It's been hard. More difficult than I could ever describe in words. But it made the three of us warriors, I believe. We are stronger and braver today than we were last month. We are forever changed. I am a different person than I was a month ago. I look at my son with determination. We can conquer anything. Though it's not because of any extraordinary power that comes from within ourselves. We are merely people. I can say with full certainty that if it weren't for God's power in my life, this month would have broken me. As a mother, I don't know if I would have survived the pain and frustration of all that the past month brought. I don't know how any mother could. Not without God. Not without His grace. But His grace is sufficient. It was sufficient for me this month. It was sufficient for my little family. It brought us through. It saw us through our darkest hour. We didn't just merely survive. We thrived because God's precious grace lifted us up to soar on wings like eagles. (Isaiah 40:31) That's what God's grace does.

I pray that my life has been and will continue to be a living sacrifice to the true and holy God. It's not what I asked for. If He chose to give me what I'd asked for I would be no more than ordinary. I wouldn't be used. I would blend into the background of the world. But God saw fit to use me and my family and no matter the circumstances, I can truly be thankful and give Him glory and praise for that. Today, one month later, I am thankful that sometimes God doesn't give us a choice. Sometimes He allows things to happen when He wants to use us that we would naturally choose not to go through. If God asked me today, I would say no. I'm a mother and I would never choose for my son to hurt or to be sick. But I'm thankful for the victory that God has won. And you know what's amazing? He knew what was going to happen all along. He knew, even in our darkest hour, even when my tears were falling and I was begging him on my knees, He knew even then that I would sit here one month later and write to my friends and brothers and sisters in Christ that Jack is home and all is well. He won the victory a LONG time ago. What a MIGHTY God we serve.

"For I know the plans I have for you," declares the Lord. "Plans to prosper you and not harm you. Plans to give you hope and a future."

JEREMIAH 29:11

"But those who put their hope in the Lord will renew their strength. They will soar on wings like eagles. They will run and not grow weary. They will walk and not be faint."

ISAIAH 40:31

FRIDAY, JULY 13, 2012

Time Marches On:
Two Months Post-Op

"Praise him—he is your God, and you have seen with your own
eyes the great and astounding things that he has done for you."

DEUTERONOMY 10:21

We've had a really calm few weeks. I can't even believe that in three days it will be two months since surgery. Time marches on.

Jack has finally reached the point of full recovery. His scar healed up so much better than I could have imagined. I really love it. That probably sounds crazy but to me it's his badge of war and he will wear it proudly. On June 21, we had a clinic visit and Jack's cardiologist told us that he could come off of oxygen. He had us continue to monitor Jack's sats from home and he did great. Sats didn't change at all. That was a BIG day for us. We celebrated with quite a few tears,.. mostly mine. At the six week mark we started being able to pick him up under his arms again which was kind of the last milestone we were trying to reach. We were extra cautious at first but now he's back to being thrown into the air like every other little boy. It makes him giggle which makes my heart smile. He's back up to six ounces of breastmilk. He's actually eating so much that I can hardly keep up. But this heart mommy knows that this is not a bad problem to have. He is all smiles and giggles these days. He loves his feet so much and he can almost sit up by himself. He reaches for everything and chews on anything he can get into his little mouth. His two teeth are adorable and he drools and chews enough to make me believe that we might see a few more teeth pretty soon. He has absolutely no developmental delays. For the most part, he's perfectly normal.

We went to clinic yesterday where Jack had an ECHO and then we talked with his cardiologist. He told us that Jack's heart looks "pristine" which was beyond amazing to hear. He told us that right now we are going to focus on getting Jack off of two of his meds. We will be going down on his doses each week and we'll continue to monitor his saturations with the pulse oximeter we have at home. We don't go back to clinic for TWO WHOLE MONTHS which will be by far the longest we've been without a visit to the hospital or an ECHO. We could not have had a better report and we are SO thankful that God has seen fit to provide complete healing for our sweet boy.

We will visit Jack's pediatrician this coming Tuesday for his six month checkup and shots. We will also be working with him on getting Jack started on cereal and baby food soon. He wanted us to wait on this step with Jack because he needed as much breast milk as possible right now because his immune system took a major hit when he got sick in the hospital and then had to be on so many antibiotics.

Two days ago we celebrated Jack's six month birthday. I can NOT believe that six months has already passed since the day that I held my sweet boy for the first time. This past six months have been the most amazing and most challenging months of my life. I have learned more about myself, my marriage, my family, my community, and my God than I have in my entire life. And let me tell you friends, they are all GOOD. There were moments during each different hospital stay, from the time spent in the RNICU when Jack was born to the time spent in the CICU after surgery where I felt like time was standing still. I longed for the day when I could look over at my son and know that his first surgery was behind us and he was okay. To see him playing and laughing. To not look at him in fear of what was ahead. I told my sister today that for Jack's whole short little life so far, there hasn't been a day that has passed that I didn't carry the weight of the fear of losing him to this disease. My fear was crippling and overwhelming. But today I can truly say that I am not afraid. We are finally passed the hardest step. Yes, Jack still has one more surgery to go and I know that it will be every bit as difficult for us to face when the time comes. But I am choosing not to focus on that right now. I am going to live in this moment and celebrate what God has done, knowing that He will certainly do it again next time around. Because I know in my heart that God's plan for Jack goes far beyond a few short months or years. His plan for Jack is bigger than battling heart disease, and I have vowed to do my part to raise him to be the extraordinary person that he was created to be so that God can continue to use his life in an extraordinary way for many, many wonderful years to come.

I'm so thankful for every single prayer that has been laid before the feet of our almighty God on behalf of my precious son and my little family. My heart is overwhelmed at the amount of grace that has been poured out over my life and the lives of my husband and son. God is so merciful and so good. His love is overwhelming and unfathomable. I pray that He receives every ounce of glory that comes from our story. And when you say your prayers tonight, you thank him for us too. Thank him for saving our boy. Thank him for saving us all.

"Now to him who is able to do immeasurably more than all we ask or imagine, according to his power that is at work within us."

EPHESIANS 3:20

PART 2

THE FONTAN

After Jack's Glenn surgery and recovery, life eventually bounced back to "normal" for us. Once he came off of the oxygen, eventually the equipment company came and picked up all of the equipment from our house. Life began to move forward without hesitation. Jack and I spent our days at home together while Josh was at work. He continued to grow and we made our regular cardiology visits. Those visits began to grow fewer and farther between with good news each and every time. Jack was growing and healing, and so were we. One at a time Jack was taken off of all of the medications he had been on. We went from medication all day everyday and a kitchen counter that doubled as a pharmacy, to one single baby aspirin at night before bedtime. Throwing away mountains of prescription bottles was a freeing and gratifying experience. God had blessed us and all of the fear and darkness seemed to be behind us.

In January 2013, we celebrated the first birthday of a happy, chunky, thriving little boy who had overcome more obstacles already in his little life than most will face in an entire lifetime. We gathered at the end of his Mickey Mouse Clubhouse birthday party to release balloons in honor of the time we spent at the feet of Jesus on his behalf and we gathered in the driveway to say thank you to He who is more than able for the gift of healing that we had received.

We opened our door to visitors at last, I took a new teaching job and life began to feel like the life we had pictured before that fateful day that we were told that Jack's heart was not whole. Jack grew. He thrived. And we did our best not to look too far back or too far forward, though we knew that our journey with congenital heart disease was far from over. We visited the cardiology clinic once every six months and though we always received good news about the current state of Jack's health, I always felt myself being compelled to ask about the Fontan. The Fontan was the second part of the surgery series that Jack's heart required. It was the completion of the new circulation system that they were giving to him which would allow his heart to last longer. At around 4 years old, we got our answer. The time had come and Jack was ready for the next step.

Jack played t-ball. Not well, I might add. But he played nonetheless. Mostly for me because he just looked so darn cute in that little baseball outfit. Sometimes we dragged him out onto the field kicking and screaming with promises of gummies and juice if he would stay for a while and not cause too much of a scene. Other times he went happily onto the field, only to face the fence and play in the dirt, completely oblivious to the game that was taking place around him. Anytime he misbehaved others would say, "don't be too hard on him... look at all he's been through." This was the picture of our "normal" that we had so desperately craved. Our son, on the baseball field with all the other kids. Our son in the kid's choir at church with all the other kids. But still, the dark cloud of the Fontan loomed over me, casting a shadow on everything we did. I struggled with bitterness, sadness and fear of what the future held for us.

Finally a date was chosen and written on the calendar. May 26, 2016. Time had passed much faster than I could have ever imagined that it would and though life brought us unimaginable joy during those 4 years in-between, we still always knew what our future held. Life, as normal as we could have ever hoped for it to be, was still colored by the heaviness that was another open-heart surgery on the road ahead. We could never even pretend to forget that the last time we handed our seemingly healthy baby boy over to the doctors with the hope of healing, he almost didn't come back out of that hospital with us. Logically, we knew there was no choice in the matter. The surgery was his only option. But knowing that fact did not make the weeks and days leading up to surgery any easier.

Trading Fear for Peace

"I have told you these things, so that in me you may have peace. In this world you will have trouble. But take heart! I have overcome the world."

JOHN 16:33

Peace.

Peace is something that we all take for granted until we need it. When we need it, peace can be hard to come by. I see people that I love struggling to find peace in their lives and I know that my heart knows the magnitude of its value more than most.

With Jack's next surgery just around the corner, I've been struggling lately to find peace. Everyone tells me that it's natural to be scared after what we went through last time. Jack's Glenn surgery didn't go as planned. It was, by far, the scariest time of our lives. There were moments when we didn't know if we were going to get to bring our baby home. He got so sick. His heart didn't respond like other kids' hearts usually do And he was just a baby then.

This time around he's four years old. A little person. He's got his own, larger-than-life personality. He's wild and fearless and spoiled rotten. He loves to play and watch videos on YouTube. He LOVES his baby brother. He's simply wonderful. He fills our days with joy and laughter and I honestly don't know who or where we would be without him.

All of that just makes this time around that much harder. This time I'm not just scared of surgery. Don't get me wrong. I'm very scared of surgery. More scared than I could possibly express. But there is an additional element this time that we didn't have to deal with last time. This time he's not just a baby. He's our little boy. And how do we even begin to tell him what he is about to face? He is about to experience more pain and more fear than most experience in a lifetime. And nothing about that is fair.

One thing I learned about life the day that my son was born is that life is just not fair sometimes. Sometimes there is no rhyme or reason. Sometimes you just have to give it to God and know that even though He doesn't want the pain for us, He can still use it to make us into what He created us to be. Because there is one thing I know for sure... God does not want us to be afraid.

"I have told you these things, so that in me you may have peace. In this world you will have trouble. But take heart! I have overcome the world." John 16:33

Fear is a part of our human nature. But that doesn't mean that we should allow ourselves to succumb to it. Part of our journey as Christians is to submit to Him daily, even when we don't know His plan. Even when His plan might not line up with our plan. His word says He will never leave us or forsake us. That means that He is always with us. He's with us in the darkest moments. He's with us on the brightest days. Always is always.

God doesn't say that we might possibly have trouble. He says that we WILL have trouble. Sin turned God's perfect creation into a fallen world and because of that, we all experience trouble from time to time. Regardless of the trouble that we face though, we know that God can pour peace into our spirits if we will only allow Him to do so.

Now let me just tell you... I can hold onto my fears just as tightly as the next person. Believe me. There are nights where I just want to cry all night. I just want to let it out and embrace the darkness. It is what our human nature tells us to do. Cry. Feel sorry for yourself. You don't deserve this. And I would be lying if I told you that I don't do it. I give in. I cry. I get crazy and have anxiety attacks and my poor, sweet husband has to calm me down and remind me to breathe again. But that is not the way that God wants us to handle our fear. He doesn't want us to let fear have our hearts. He wants us to give our fear to Him and let Him exchange it for peace.

Sounds easy, right? Here God. You take this awful situation and give me peace and tell me that it's all going to be fine and I'll just go on with my life like it isn't happening.

Nope. That's just denial. I do that sometimes too.

Exchanging fear for peace is much more than just pretending like your fear isn't there. It's truly learning to trust God to handle the situation. And it's hard.

Exchanging fear for peace is hard because it takes time and work. You have to dedicate yourself to God's Word and to prayer and you have to be vulnerable to Him and His will for your life. You have to relinquish control. And anyone who knows me at all knows that I am not good at giving up control of anything. In fact, I would venture to say that my friends and family would probably call me a control freak. So giving God complete control is always a work in progress. And I mess it up and take my fears back all the time. I'm certainly no example to follow in this area. It's something I'm working on though. It's something God is working on within me. And I'm thankful for the lessons, though they are difficult ones to learn.

"God is our refuge and strength, an ever-present help in times of trouble." -Psalm 46:1

God's plan is already in place. He already sees the light on the other side of the darkness that stands in front of us. And He stands between the darkness and us and He shields us because He is our refuge. He pours His strength into our veins and breathes His peace into our hearts as we walk through to the other side. Then He heals the wounds that are left and leaves us only with scars that remind us who we once were and how far He has brought us.

WEDNESDAY, MARCH 2, 2016
Pre-Fontan Heart Cath

"This is the confidence we have in approaching God: that
if we ask anything according to His will, He hears us."

1 JOHN 5:14

It's been almost 4 years since Jack's last surgery. Everything has changed so much that when we look back on that time in the hospital, it almost doesn't even feel real anymore. We've known for a long time that this spring was going to be the time for Jack's next surgery. It's been a dark cloud looming over our heads for years, but its always been so far into the future that it felt like we had plenty of time.

The last time we saw Dr. Law for Jack's 6-month check-up he said that everything looked good and asked us if we were ready to start talking about scheduling his next surgery. With Jack's heart doing so good after his last surgery, there was never any immediate need for him to have his next one so it was always pretty much left up to us. We could decide when it was best for our family. Of course, I always wanted Dr. Law to just tell us what he thought was best. Eventually, after a lot of talking, praying, and waiting we decided that this coming summer would be best. That way he will have plenty of time to recover and get back to his normal self before he starts to kindergarten next year.

Dr. Law told us that we would schedule his cath for February and then surgery around the end of May so that I could be home with him for the entire summer during his recovery.

We got the call to schedule the cath about two months ago. February 17th. It was on a Wednesday. Then, while I was in Disney World with the cheerleaders I got the prep call. That's the call where they tell you all about what to expect, when he can eat and drink, what to bring, etc. That's when it started to feel real.

The week leading up to the procedure was full of fear, extra kisses, long talks, and tears. (All of the tears and fear came from Mommy, Jack was always brave and ready.) We talked to Jack a lot about the upcoming procedure. We never want him to be taken by surprise when we walk into a hospital and hand him to strangers. We want him to understand what's happening and why. We explained as much as we could both about his extra special heart and what was going to happen when we went to the hospital. He was excited because we told him he would get lots of "prizes" when he woke up from surgery. We prayed with him and for him a thousand times. We listened to his sweet voice pray for himself.

The night before the procedure we took Harrison to Nonna's for a sleepover. We were going to have to be at the hospital very early the next morning so we decided it was best if baby brother spent the night with Nonna so we didn't have to get him up early and out in the cold. Once we dropped him off we took Jack to his favorite place to eat—Cabos. He was wild and silly and sweet as always. We talked some more about surgery and prayed over him together before he fell asleep.

The next morning we woke our sleepy boy up and drove to Children's. They told us to pack an overnight bag just in case and Jack filled half of our suitcase with toys. When we got there they checked us in and put us in a room. Two very sweet nurses came in and explained what was going to happen and then Dr. Law came in and talked to us about the procedure and what he was going to do. He explained the risks. Then he said they would take him back for the procedure in about half an hour. Just after he left our family came in. Then the nurses came in to give Jack a dose of Versed and Tylenol. Little did we know at that time that giving him that medicine would be the worst part of the day. It took all four of us (two nurses and me and Josh) to hold him down and force the medicine down. He HATED it. Once they got the Versed in they told him the Tylenol would be "yummy". When they started to force the Tylenol in he loudly informed them that it was in fact "NOT YUMMY!!"

Once that part was over we picked him up and loved on him. Then the nurse practitioner came in to ask questions for his chart. It was about 4 minutes after the medicine went down when Jack's little head started to slide backward off of Josh's shoulder. He literally couldn't hold his own head up. Then he started to giggle. Silly giggles that I had never heard before. He was drunk as a skunk. We all laughed at him until we cried. He got sillier as the minutes passed and by the time the nurse practitioner left our room he was slurring his words and dropping every toy he tried to pick up. It was a much-needed moment of relief from the tension and stress where we all just watched him and laughed.

At around 7:30 a group of nurses came in to tell us it was time. Our family walked out to the waiting room and Josh carried Jack as they wheeled his empty bed back to the OR. When we got to the door- that was as far as we could go—they said it was time for us to hand him over. He was still very silly-headed and sleepy-eyed but he looked up and reached for me. I grabbed his little limp hand and told him I loved him and would see him soon. Josh handed him to a very tiny doctor who could barely hold the weight of his limp-noodle body. They went around the corner and the doors closed behind them. I cried for a while in the hallway and then we went and sat in his room by ourselves for a few minutes while I got myself together.

Then we went to meet our family in the waiting room where we spent the next 3+ hours. We sat and sat and sat. Finally, after what felt like years, the nurse came out and said that me and Josh could go back now. We waited in his room and Dr. Law came in. He said that everything looked great. He was all smiles. He said Jack did really well and was resting in recovery now. He said they did have to coil one collateral vessel. But other than that it went well and Jack's heart was looking exceptionally good for his particular CHD. He said we had the official green light to move forward with the Fontan.

{Collateral vessels are abnormal blood vessels that connect the aorta with the pulmonary arteries. The aorta is a blood vessel that carries blood from the heart to arteries throughout the body. Pulmonary arteries are the vessels that transfer blood from the heart back to the lungs for oxygen.

Everyone has collateral vessels, but they're normally small and not in use. They become enlarged in some people with congenital heart disease (heart disease that's present since birth). When a collateral vessel enlarges, it may let blood flow from an artery to an adjacent artery or it may carry blood downstream and then back to the same artery.

Collateral vessels can make the heart work harder and in some cases should be closed. These vessels can cause other medical conditions, such as myocardial ischemia, an insufficient blood supply to the middle muscular layer of the heart wall; congestive heart failure or the weakening of the heart; endocarditis, an infection of the heart's inner lining; stroke, caused by a lack of blood to the brain; and aneurysms, which are bulging or ballooning of a blood vessel wall. Collateral vessels affect children and adults and can be a congenital or acquired heart defect.

During cardiac catheterization a doctor inserts thin, flexible tubes called catheters into a vein in the leg or neck and threads them through the vein to the heart. Once in the heart, the catheters are used as conduits to place small metal coils or plugs in the collateral vessels. The coil causes a blood clot to form and close the vessel. Over time, tissue grows around the coil, forming a permanent seal.}

Josh and I waited in Jack's room around half an hour until a nurse finally came in and said that he was doing really great in recovery. She said he was awake and happy and was eating a purple popsicle. It was another twenty minutes or so until they wheeled him out of recovery and back to us. He was awake and happy to see us. He was still eating his popsicle. He looked so good. They told us he had to lie flat for six hours but that the procedure had gone so well that when the six hours was up we could take him home.

Josh went and got our family and they all came in to see him and bring him TONS of prizes. He got toys and books and puzzles and games. He was happy. He never once complained. The nurses came in and out taking his vitals and looking at his dressings. He was patient and brave. They came in to do an x-ray and said we had to leave the room. I stood outside the door and watched as he did every single thing they told him to do. He was so big.

We got to look at the x-ray and see the coil. It's HUGE. His little heart is so small and the coil looked giant in comparison but I know that it was necessary and will help his heart so I just had to accept it as a good thing. It will help Jack get the blood flow that he needs.

We really didn't think that Jack would lie flat even for one hour but he laid on that bed like a champion for SIX SOLID HOURS! We played with him and read to him and he watched YouTube videos. Time went by quickly. The crazy part was that he hated lying there. It wasn't like he was lying flat because he was satisfied. He didn't like it but he was so big and so mature that he knew he had to so he just did.

Where did my baby go? When did I get this big boy that lets doctors poke on him and lies flat just because we told him to? No tears all evening. Brave doesn't even begin to cover it. The only explanation for it was God. He was there and He made a way. And we could not be more thankful.

As always, a million thanks to everyone who lifted him (and us) up in prayer that day. We felt calm and peace and knew that God was answering the prayers of a multitude and we are forever grateful.

FRIDAY, MAY 20, 2016

In Oceans Deep

"When you pass through the waters, I will be with you; and when you pass through the rivers, they will not sweep over you. When you walk through the fire, you will not be burned; the flames will not set you ablaze."

ISAIAH 43:2

It's hard to make yourself believe that the fire won't set you ablaze when you can see the fire coming right for you. There's nowhere to run, nowhere to hide. No-one who can stand between you and the fire. It's your fire. And you have to walk into it. And you have to trust that it won't take you down.

There are some days when I know I have the faith of David. The kind of faith that says bring it on Goliath. I'm not scared. Then some days David-like-faith is harder to come by. There are days when I can take a deep breath and step into the furnace 100% sure that I'm ready for whatever may come. But there are other days when the furnace is Goliath and I am NOT David.

It's easy to sing Oceans. To praise the God of the universe and know in my heart that He is sovereign and He LOVES me. But to stand before Him and ASK Him to lead me where my trust is without borders... Let me tell you friend, you better know what you're asking before you say those words out loud with true conviction. Because He will. And it will be glorious. But that glory lives on the other side of the fire. And there is only one way to get there.

In our journey with Jack we have experienced many scary days. However, undoubtedly this day four years ago takes the cake. The day Jack crashed. It was four days post-op after his Glenn surgery. It was just like a scene from Grey's Anatomy. But real. And my baby. And horrifying. And there was no by-passing that fire. As I read back over the events that took place during Jack's post-op hospital stay after the Glenn I'm reminded of all of the bad things that happened. Everyday seemed to bring worse news than the day before. Ultimately I remember the night when he started throwing up blood. I'm no doctor but I know what that means. We were at the end of the line. And the doctors weren't confident that they would find a solution to all of Jack's issues in time to save him.

You don't know fear until you've faced the possibility of losing one of your children. (And for my precious friends who have lived through that nightmare, my love and my heart and my daily prayers for continued strength go out to you.) I wish I could say that I can't imagine, but unfortunately, I can.

I think a lot of times we draw a line in the sand for God. Here Lord, you can have all of these things. Use me any way you want. But these things here behind the line… they're mine. Don't touch them. And let me just tell you… My kids… They aren't anywhere near that line.

But the truth is that the love that we have for our children that feels so deep and so heavy that sometimes the fear of losing them or seeing them get hurt suffocates us, God loves US so much more than that. And when He takes us by the hand and walks us toward the fire, He has a purpose. And it's always for our own good. After all, this life is not about this life at all. It's about our eternal life with Him. For today, we're just passing through. And the more we build our faith in Him and allow Him to use us to lead others to Him, the more glory there will be for us when we get to the other side.

> *"Spirit lead me where my trust is without borders*
> *Let me walk upon the waters, wherever you would call me*
> *Take me deeper than my feet could ever wander,*
> *and my faith will be made stronger,*
> *in the presence of my Savior"*

So for today, I'm doing my best to keep my eyes above the waves and to remember that I am His, and He is mine. His plan for Jack far exceeds this chapter of his story. I'm thankful to be used in even a small way but His plan for Jack is BIG. And I can't wait to see what He has in store for him on the other side of this fire.

WEDNESDAY, MAY 25, 2016

One Day Pre-Op

"The Lord will fight for you. You need only be still."

EXODUS 14:14

Our bags are packed and I think we are about as ready as we're ever going to be. Today was great. We got to take a tour of the hospital to see all of the different places we will be throughout our stay. Jack got to meet Lego Man and they gave him a really cool box of Jake and the Neverland Pirates Lego Duplos and a cool Lego picture frame for his picture with Lego Man. He was SUPER brave for all of his pre-op testing. He only cried once and that was for the awful blood work! All of the nurses and doctors that we met were wonderful and treated Jack like he was the ONLY kid on the planet! He loved all of the attention! Once we were done there we came home to spend one last afternoon with brother before we have to be away from him for a little while. Now Jack is out on the golf cart with his daddy, Harrison is asleep for the night, and I am taking a break from packing to get all of my last pre-Fontan thoughts out.

So here is how tomorrow will go...

We will arrive at Children's at 6am and check in. They will take Jack back to a pre-op room where we will meet with his surgeon, anesthesiologist, and other doctors to go over what all they will do. We already know most of it and got a chance to ask question today but tomorrow is a one-more-time, just-in-case kind of deal. In the meantime he will get a dose of Versed to make him loopy so that he won't mind going with the doctors when it's time to go back. At around 7:00 they'll let our family flood his room to give hugs and kisses and say see-you-later. Then they will allow Josh and I to walk him to the OR doors. Then we have to say our own see-you-laters. Once they're back there they will put Jack under using a mask. He will experience no pain at all. Once he's under they will start to run his lines and get him prepped. Prep takes around an hour. Once they're ready to begin they will call us and let us know. We will be in the waiting room with our family and friends. The second call will come when they're ready to put Jack onto bypass. The goal is for him to stay on bypass for 45 minutes or less but it could take up to an hour. We're praying that they don't have any bleeds (like last time) that would cause him to have to stay on bypass longer than necessary. We'll get a third call when they're ready to take him off of bypass and start his heart back up. They'll call once more when the surgery is over and they are ready to close him up. Closing up can take hours because they will be sewing layers together. Once Dr. Dabal is done he will come out and meet with Josh and I and tell us about the surgery. When Jack is done they will move him to his room in the CICU. Once he is all set up in his room Josh and I will be able to see him. They told us today that we should expect for him to be intubated and sedated for most, if not all of the first day. They will attempt to extubate him either tomorrow night or Friday morning. Please pray for his saturations to SOAR so that he can breathe on his own. This was our biggest challenge last time around but we are believing fully for a better outcome this time around.

No one will be allowed to see Jack tomorrow after surgery except for me and Josh. This is for his safety as he will be in a very critical state. Once he has had time to be taken off the vent and woken up we will allow our immediate family members to come back and see him. They told us to expect to be there for at least a week but not to be surprised if we stay longer than that. In our experience anything less than a month is a blessing so we will just take it a day at a time.

We are praying and believing for a miracle. We trust God to provide Jack with an exceptional surgery tomorrow and an amazing and quick recovery. Our faith is in a God who can move mountains. All glory and honor and praise to Him regardless of what lies ahead for us.

THURSDAY, MAY 26, 2016

Fontan Day

"I will give thanks to you, Lord, with all my heart;
I will tell of all your wonderful deeds."

PSALM 9:1

We had a really rough night last night. Jack accidentally smashed his little finger in the car door and it hurt him really badly. He cried on and off all night and hardly slept at all. The only way I could get him to rest was to sit with him on the couch in the living room. We watched Jake and the Neverland Pirates until he fell asleep. I couldn't sleep anyway so it didn't bother me to sit up with him. I just hated to see him hurting and we couldn't give him any medicine or even milk for comfort. I got up at 4am and got ready to go. We woke Jack up at 5 and took him straight to the car in his jammies. My Aunt Jeanie came to spend the day with Harrison.

We checked in at 6am. A TON of our family was already here to see Jack this morning before he went back. He got to give most everyone a kiss and a hug before they gave him the Versed. We got to talk with Dr. Dabal about what to expect and ask any last minute questions. At 7:30 they came to take him to the OR. Josh and I stopped to pray for him and he giggled the whole time. They let me walk with him to the OR doors and then I had to hand him over. He clung to me but was silly-headed because of the Versed so when I handed him over he wasn't too upset. We watched them round the corner. It was a difficult moment for us to say the least.

Once we got back out to the waiting room I ran to the bathroom to let some tears fall and then came back out to a sweet surprise... Two of the nurses who took care of Jack after his first surgery were waiting to see me. Heather was just heading out but Ashley was going to be in and out with us all day! That brought me so much comfort. She also reassured me that Jack's nurse Amanda was going to be super sweet to him! This helped lift my spirits and get me back together.

They took a long time to make that first call (that he was under and they were going to start the procedure) and I started to panic so I went to the desk and the sweet receptionist called them for me. It just so happened that they were about to make the first cut. It was time. So we settled in and waited. The second call came to tell us he was doing great and they got through the bone easily. The third call told us that he was going onto bypass. Next call- 45 minutes later on the dot- said that he was coming off of bypass and things were going great. Last call said that the hard part was over and they were going to close up. It was a long morning filled with nerves and anxiety but also peace. God-given peace for all of us waiting out there. He sailed through perfectly.

Dr. Dabal met us in the conference room. He said that everything went wonderfully. There wasn't much scar tissue at all. He said that Jack's DKS (one of the procedures that they performed on his heart during his first open-heart surgery at 4 months old) was perfect and belongs in textbooks. He said that they didn't have to do a fenestration because Jack's heart function looked good. They didn't have to stop his heart at all this time. He went on to say that Jack's anatomy is ideal for the Fontan circulation and he thinks that Jack is going to do great in the future. He said that they talked about how great Jack's anatomy is while they were in the OR and that if you have to have a kid born with a single ventricle heart, Jack's is one you would want to have! He told us that even though Jack's heart won't last until he's 80, he feels confident that it will get him well into adulthood and that by the time that he needs a transplant there is no telling what they will be able to do for him. What beautiful words to hear. He even joked and said that I didn't look like I believed him. I just said that this is just a different ballgame than what we're used to and it's hard to take in all of the positive news. My human nature wants to doubt and find the negative but today it was all good news friends.

It was about another hour before we got to see him. When Josh and I rounded the corner my heart sang. My baby. Finally. Alive and done with surgery. We're not out of the woods yet but it sure is nice to know that they've closed his chest up for the last time, for a good while at least. We had really prepared ourselves for what he would look like. After his Glenn he was very swollen and hooked to more monitors and machines than I could count. This time he just looked like my Jack, asleep, intubated, but Jack. My heart.

Josh and I sat at his bedside for an hour or so until he started to wake up. He opened his eyes and looked at me. He was uncomfortable and seemed scared so they gave him some medicine to help with the pain and he fell back asleep. Later he woke up a little more and they got him ready to extubate. It only took a few seconds and the tube was out. Last time he was intubated for WEEKS. This time, hours. Wow. What miracles our God still does. He was happy to have the tube out of his mouth and instantly started asking for juice. They told him if he could wait a while they would give him some ice chips. That's not what he wanted but he said he would take it. He let the nurse give him one or two before he took the cup from her and started chomping down. I told Josh I've never heard someone's chewing sound so beautiful! He got to drink some water a little bit later. Dr. Dabal said that we have to take it extra slow with Fontan kids because the new circulation of blood (bypassing the heart and going straight to the lungs) causes his other organs to have to adjust and drinking too much too fast might make him sick.

Right now it's 4:30pm and I can't believe that all of this happened today. I couldn't have written a better possible story for Jack's surgery day. All of the stress, anxiety and tears leading up to this day and God knew all along that He was going to bless us with the best possible surgery day. It is my sincerest of hopes that ALL of the glory from this day will bypass us and go straight to Him. Jack is strong because God is funneling strength into him. Josh and I are making it because He is pouring His grace over us every single second. He deserves every ounce of the glory.

FRIDAY, MAY 27, 2016
Post-Op Day One

"But he said to me, "My grace is sufficient for you, for my power is made perfect in weakness." Therefore I will boast all the more gladly about my weaknesses, so that Christ's power may rest on me."

2 CORINTHIANS 12:9

Jack had a fairly uneventful night last night. He woke up every 20–30 minutes but would fall back to sleep pretty quickly. He slept for a solid 3 hours from 4–7am. Dr. Dabal came by this morning and said everything was looking great and that Jack was doing really well. Physical therapy came by pretty early and asked Jack if he wanted to get out of the bed. He had been wanting to get out of bed all morning so he was more than willing to go with her to the bathroom. It was a rather big undertaking considering all of the tubes and wires that are connected to him. They had to get him hooked to a portable oxygen tank and cap off all of his IV's and tubes to get us to the bathroom. I stood in front of him and held his hands while the physical therapist, the nurse, and Josh all lifted him off the bed and onto the floor a little at a time. He walked with me then, holding both hands, all the way to the potty. He pee peed really good and then walked all the way back. By the time we made it back to the bed he was exhausted and needed to get comfortable and rest.

His pain has been rough today. He is really struggling with the chest tubes. He hasn't mentioned his actual incision one time… It's all about those tubes. Several friends told us to expect that. The tubes are very painful and once the tubes come out, your baby will come alive again. The problem is that the tubes are for the fluid that is draining and Jack has a TON of drainage. Dr. Dabal told us that we could expect to stay 2-3 weeks just waiting for the draining to stop because most Fontan patients experience a significant amount of fluid drainage. Basically, the tubes will be the last thing to go before we can take him home. Yuck.

At around 3 this afternoon we got the green light to move to the step-down unit. You can't imagine how surprising and over-whelmingly amazing that felt. Jack stayed in the CICU for over 3 weeks last time around. To leave the CICU after one ONE DAY this time has been unreal. We don't know how to act! When we got to our new room we realized that here Jack doesn't have to be attached to so many monitors! He has his two chest tubes, his main line in his groin, another line in his hand, his oxygen, his sat monitor, and his heart monitor. We got rid of his arterial line before we left and got to say goodbye to his oxygen shortly after getting to the new room. And he is satting a BEAUTIFUL 90 on NO OXYGEN! Praise Jesus!!

Since getting to the floor Jack hasn't been able to keep any-thing down. We've tried milk twice and he threw it up both times. He has thrown up about 4-5 times total, sometimes just dry heaving because there is nothing in him to throw up. Tonight he is holding down a few sips of gatorade. BUT he has been pee peeing pretty consistently so he's not dehydrating just yet. We're going to keep pushing the gatorade slowly and hope that it stays down!

In the grand scheme of things Jack is recovering perfectly. His saturations are holding strong in the low 90's. His color looks amazing. He got to come off of oxygen and his IV drip.

Right now it's a waiting game. We're just watching the fluid drain and hoping that it slows down. It's beyond hard to watch him in all of this pain but ultimately the pain is temporary and will go away. The bottom line is that our baby is done. The surgery that has been living in our thoughts and dreams for the past 4 years is over. Day by day he will get better. Before we know it he will be back to running and playing and this time he won't get winded as easily and he will be even harder to keep up with! And, God willing, it will be YEARS and YEARS before we have to face anything like this again!

God has really shown up and shown out this time. I can't even really wrap my brain around it. Before Jack's Glenn surgery when he was a baby I used to sit in the floor next to his cradle with my hand between the bars holding onto his little foot and crying and begging God to save him. I was so scared of that surgery. I didn't know if we would ever get to bring him home again. And let me tell you friends, it was a long hard road. God didn't let me go in expecting it to be easy because He knew it wasn't going to be. He prepared my heart.

And this time around in that same way He prepared my heart again. But this time, I had peace. I can't even explain it. After what we went through last time I should have been terrified. And I would be lying if I said that I wasn't scared. I cried my fair share of fearful tears. But the Holy Spirit was there. Holding me together. Telling me to let go of my fear. That it was all going to be okay. So much so that when I was praying about the surgery there were times when I couldn't even find words to say. I just found myself telling God that I needed Him to help me trust Him. I wanted to just lay it at his feet and I needed SO MUCH GRACE to be able to do that. And y'all, He gave it to me. Seriously. He did. I can't explain it. I just felt so much peace and assurance that this time would be different. Not because we deserved an easier road because last time was hard. Not because Jack was older and stronger. Just because God was speaking peace into my spirit. I could feel it in my bones. This time would be different.

There is no time when you will find yourself closer to God than when you face the unimaginable. So many people tell me that they can't imagine what we're going through or how hard it must be. That's true. If I had two perfectly healthy boys I would think the same thing. But God just gives you what you need when you need it. He doesn't even wait for you to ask for it. That's what grace is. It's God moving inside you, giving you comfort and peace and strength when you didn't even know you needed it. I can't credit the strength and the peace to myself. I'm a human, a mom no less. I'm a mess over my kids. Jack stubs his toe and I fall apart. No, this is ALL GOD. None me. And the way that He works within us, pouring His grace over us and then doesn't even demand the credit. I mean, I could take all the credit and be all, look how strong and brave I'm being, and he probably wouldn't even zap me down with a lightning bolt. I mean, I don't know for sure but I don't think He does that usually. He just fills us up with whatever we need in the moment and then watches us walk in peace because He loves us so much. He wants to see us at peace. I guess that's where grace began.

PS- Brother came to visit us today and we finally got our first sort-of smile out of Jack. I knew H would be the one to bring his smile back! They love each other so much!

SATURDAY, MAY 28, 2016

Post-op Day 2

"And God is able to bless you abundantly, so that in all things at all times, having all that you need, you will abound in every good work."

2 CORINTHIANS 9:8

Jack had a really rough night last night. He threw up all night long. He was so thirsty so we would give him a little juice or water to help clean out his mouth each time and then half an hour later he was throwing up again. He would sit up and say, "I'm about to throw up. Go get the nurse." Sweet boy.

This morning he woke up really struggling with pain. He was not as responsive to us as he was yesterday. There were some times when he was just staring off into space and not answering any of the questions we asked him. Then other times he would wake up thrashing around and yelling that it hurt. He would wake up yelling STOP!! I think that the pain surprised him when he woke up and he thought someone was doing something to him even when we weren't standing next to his bed. He's also been yelling out "Oh my God!" over and over. That is something he gets in trouble for at home because he knows he's not supposed to say that but it's not exactly easy to get onto your baby when he's screaming in pain in a hospital bed. So we have just lightly corrected him and reminded him that we say gosh or goodness, or my personal favorite—Mylanta!

This afternoon he took a turn for the SLEEPY! He has pretty much slept all evening. He has woken up to get some juice or water or to stand up to pee pee but other than that he's been out like a light all afternoon. We're sincerely hoping that doesn't mean that he'll be a party animal all night.

He asked me for a juice box about an hour ago and so I got him a new one and held it up to his mouth. He asked me for the wings so I attempted to get the wings out and ended up squeezing the juice box and spilling juice on his bed. Me and Josh both laughed and then Jack SMILED. WITH TEETH! Yay for small victories!

His drainage has slowed down some throughout the day but there is a big possibility that it's only because he has been lying down all day. Hopefully the fluid is slowing down though and we can talk about getting one, if not both of his tubes out tomorrow or in the next few days. Until the tubes come out our days will probably look a lot like today did. Just lying in bed and drinking sips of juice or water. Once the tubes are out is when we can really start getting him up and about and maybe even talk about him taking a bite or two of a cracker. Baby steps.

Even though Jack is in a lot of pain right now and doesn't seem to be making great strides in progress, the reality is that this is only post-op day 2. He's off the vent, off of oxygen, and satting in the upper 90s. Every time I look at that monitor I just smile from ear to ear. My baby boy. Finally pink. The hard part is over. Surgery went well and now we're just in recovery. It won't last forever. Everyday it will get better until he's back on the ball field or running in the yard with his friends.

SUNDAY, MAY 29, 2016
Post-Op Day 3

"And so we know and rely on the love God has for us. God is love. Whoever lives in love lives in God, and God in them."

1 JOHN 4:16

Jack had a rather uneventful night last night. He was up the first half of the night with some pain but then got some pain meds around 1:30am and slept hard for the rest of the night. When he woke up this morning we got him up to pee pee. We made him walk all the way to the potty for the 2nd time and he screamed the entire way there and back. The chest tubes are causing him a lot of pain and more than anything, moving scares him. He knows moving hurts so he would rather stay in his bed and stay still where it doesn't hurt. BUT he did it and was so brave.

The doctor came by not long after that and told us that Jack's fluid drainage is not looking great. It's a deep yellow color and the normal flow of the fluid would be lots of red then as it slows down a little yellow until it stops. Jack had lots of red and now is having even more yellow and it is nowhere near slowing down or stopping. This is leading them to believe that Jack is experiencing something called chylothorax pleural effusions. It results from lymph formed in the digestive system called chyle accumulating in the pleural cavity. The explanation is that during the surgery a part of the lymph system was nicked and some of that lymph fluid is leaking out now. The result is that the drainage will continue and be more persistent than just normal fluid drainage from the Fontan. Dr. Dabal told us before surgery that the drainage was going to be the main issue to deal with after surgery so none of this is crazy unexpected. They can't tell just yet for certain that Jack is experiencing chylothorax because he hadn't eaten a bite of anything up until this morning. If this is what he is experiencing then once he starts eating, the fat from his food intake will turn the fluid that is draining a milky white color. Then they will know for sure that this is what Jack is experiencing. However, with how little he is eating and drinking, it could take up until tomorrow or longer for that to happen. Right now we're just treating it like normal and waiting to see what happens. Either way his fluid output has not slowed down so it doesn't look like we'll be losing either chest tube for a good little while which means we're kind of just stuck waiting.

Jack is also experiencing a few other minor issues. His doctor said that his albumin, NaCl, and IgG levels are all too low and if they continue to let them fall we will get into a dangerous zone that we want to avoid so they're treating him for each of those three issues today as well. Albumin is a protein that is found in the blood. With his levels of albumin dropping it causes the osmosis of the fluid in Jack's blood to happen easier which would mean more fluid which is what we're trying to avoid. (Hey medical friends, I could be totally jacking this up-no pun intended- but I'm doing the best I can so hang in there with me.) His NaCl level is basically his sodium intake. Since he's not eating he doesn't have enough salt floating around in him. They can't push it in his IV so we're trying to get him to eat some super salty foods. Popcorn and french fries are healthy foods of choice today. Lastly his IgG levels are low and he is having to have that supplemented also. Immunoglobulin G is an antibody found in the blood. Basically, another thing he needs that his body is not producing super well right now. They gave him some benadryl just in case he was to have a bad reaction to it and then after it had time to kick in good and strong they came back to push the IgG. The infusion started super slow and after about an hour Jack woke up needing to pee pee. When we got him uncovered to use the bathroom he started shaking really bad. His face was super red and flushed and his teeth were chattering. We called for the nurse immediately and she called the nurse practitioner who told her to stop the infusion immediately and give Jack steroids, more benadryl, and Ibuprofen. We covered him up really good and I loved on him until the shaking stopped. It didn't take long for his normal color to come back and the shaking to go away. However, a few minutes later Jack started kicking his legs violently and screaming hysterically. He was thrashing around in his bed and grabbing at all of his cords and tubes. It was scary. The nurse said she thought he was having a bad reaction to the steroid. So we got him up and got him to stand up next to the bed. He continued to yell and kick his feet. The nurse pushed morphine to calm him down and after a few minutes we set him back in his bed and covered him up and he fell back asleep. It was a very scary and overwhelming hour to say the least.

The nurse practitioner came back in to talk to us about what had happened. He said around 10% of their patients that have to have the IgG end up having a bad reaction to it so it's not super uncommon. They won't try again for several days and depending on whether or not his fluid drainage slows down, he may not need it again. The IgG is just basically a replacement of the red blood cells that he needs to fight off infections. With the massive amount of fluid he has been draining, he has lost a lot of those red blood cells and therefore has a compromised immune system. If the drainage stops then his immune system will build itself back up and all will be good. If not, then they'll need to try again with the infusion in a few days. He said if we have to try again they'll try another name brand because sometimes that makes a difference. In the meantime we need to be even more careful than normal to make sure no one brings any germs or sickness into our room. So we've decided to stop all visitations for the next few days until we can tell if he's going to get past all of this on his own or if we're going to have to keep going with the interventions.

Needless to say, after a dose of morphine and a dose of benadryl at the same time, our boy passed out cold and has been completely out of it since. He's slept like a rock all afternoon. Next time he wakes up we're going to try to get him out of the bed again one more time for the night because the more he moves around the better the fluid drains.

Jack's right upper lobe of his lung is not looking too good on his x-ray today so his sats dropped to the upper 80's and they ordered some chest PT for 4:00. But since he was in the middle of a crazy episode at 4:00 they skipped it and just came in for the first time to do it tonight. All of the lying around and sleeping is good for some healing things but bad for others. He needs to be up, moving around, coughing and talking in order to clear some of the junk from his lungs and throat. Hopefully tomorrow will be a better day and we can see him up and about a little bit more. As far as the chest PT, he didn't like it. AT ALL.

Each day is progress. Even if it feels like one step forward and two steps back, it's still one step forward so we'll take it. The VERY positive is that all of the issues we have today are fixable and not life-threatening. The negative is that we have to fix these issues to make sure that our boy gets healthy and well enough to go home. It could take a few days. It could take a few weeks. In the meantime we're all missing our H like crazy. He came today and spent a few hours with us. Jack had been missing him so bad this morning when he was awake and alert but by the time he got here Jack was already out of it and couldn't enjoy him being here. We'll try again in a few days. Mommy and Daddy's hearts are torn to have our two sweet boys in two different places. But we are exceptionally blessed to have amazing parents taking great care of our sweet baby while we stay here with Jack who needs our full and undivided attention right now. I keep telling myself that this is only temporary. It will pass and my sweet family of 4 will all be back under one roof, OUR roof, soon. God's got this.

TUESDAY, MAY 31, 2016

Post-Op Days 4 and 5

"The name of the Lord is a strong tower;
the righteous man runs into it and is safe."

PROVERBS 18:10

POST-OP DAY 4

Yesterday was a really good day for Jack. We got him up and went to the play room for the first time. He played play-doh with some friends. He was in great spirits and walked a good bit. We came back to the room after that to rest for a while but he could NOT miss the Lego Movie playing in the Room of Magic downstairs so at 3:00 we loaded him back up in his wagon and went to the movie. He loved the room and the big movie screen but about 3 minutes in he decided he was just too tired so we went back to our room to rest. He didn't take a nap ALL DAY! He talked more like himself and played some in his bed. We did stickers and played with some of his toys. He drank all of his medicines good in his milk cup so we didn't have to stress over getting him to take them anymore. His drainage was still about the same. The doctor came by and said that if the drainage doesn't slow down they will have to look at some options to find out why it is flowing so heavily. One of those is another cath, which of course we want to avoid because it means anesthesia again and taking steps backwards. So we're continuing to pray that the drainage slows down soon.

Yesterday evening after the movie Jack was really tired and in a lot of pain and he started itching. They say that is a side effect of the morphine so they gave him some benadryl in his IV. After just a couple of minutes he started going crazy. He was screaming and kicking and thrashing. He was yelling out stuff that didn't make sense. He thought he was falling and he was just lying on his back. He was scratching and pulling on every wire and cord. It was awful. BUT it was familiar. He did the same thing the night before. After they stopped the IgG infusion the night before they gave him a dose of steroids and benadryl at the same time to reverse the bad reaction he was having to the IgG infusion. He started having that same crazy reaction. We thought it was the steroids. They gave him morphine and he passed out. Well, after seeing that same response tonight we realized that he is allergic to Benadryl. So they had to give him morphine again to knock him out and let the Benadryl have time to get out of his system. Needless to say Benadryl is going on his drug allergies list! Other than that one episode it was a really good day. It's been wonderful to have his sweet and silly little personality back, even if that includes him sassing and bossing us around!

POST-OP DAY 5

Today was another really great day! Jack slept good last night since he didn't nap yesterday. He woke up a few times through the night when his nurse was in here. He still HATES the chest PT. But he's back to talking non-stop. Every nurse, doctor, physical therapist, respiratory therapist, pretty much anyone who comes in our room has to play with him and hear his stories. He's talking everyone's ears off! It's wonderful. He's smiling and laughing and getting his energy back. We went to the play room again this morning and he played with the kitchen for a little while. Then we moved to the play area in front of the big window so he could sit and play and feel the sunshine. He played blocks with his daddy and had a good time. He laughed and giggled the whole time. When he got tired we made him walk about a fourth of the way back to the room before we let him get in his wagon. We went back to the room and rested until time for the build-a-bear workshop downstairs. He could NOT miss that workshop. We loaded him back up in his wagon and headed down stairs. He got a bear and named her Madison. He doctored her all up and had a great time. He didn't want to leave when we were done! But brother was waiting on us in our room so we headed back up to see him. Jack and Harrison were both equally ecstatic to see each other! Jack's Nonna, Mimi, Shay, and Aunt Jeanie all came and brought tons of prizes for him to open. He had a great time playing with all of his new toys.

Harrison got ready for a nap and Jack was feeling tired and needing to rest so everyone decided it was time to go. Daddy decided to go home with H for the night since he's been away from us all for almost a week now. So now it's just me and Jack for the night. We're pretty much settled in for the evening. He's watching Frozen and eating Doritos. Feeling pretty good at the moment, although he's having some pain and doesn't want to drink his milk because he knows his medicine is in there!

The nurse practitioner came in and talked to me about what is going on with the tubes. She said that right now we're just in a waiting period. She said it doesn't always happen but definitely happens sometimes. The drainage is just another result of the new blood flow and Jack's body trying to get used to the new pressures. It will stop when his body is finished adjusting. The GOOD news is that his fluid never turned that milky color that is associated with the chylothorax. She said that he's been eating and drinking enough now that we should have seen a change by now if that was going to be the case. We're not 100% out of the woods with that issue but she said that she would say that it probably isn't going to change. So yay for that! No weird diet! She said that there is a possibility that we will have to have another cath if the drainage doesn't stop but that is not in our immediate future. For now and the next several days we just wait and continue to get Jack moving and keep the fluid draining. The more he moves and walks the more it will drain out of his body. He's also on a couple of medications that are meant to dry that fluid up more quickly. It's likely that we will be here for another week or so just watching the tubes drain. Our prayer of course is that it will dry up on its own without further intervention. Then Jack can continue to get better day by day and go home when they stop draining.

Post-Op Days 6, 7, and 8

"Come to me, all who labor and are heavy
laden, and I will give you rest."

MATTHEW 11:28

POST-OP DAYS 6 AND 7

The past couple of days have been really good days for Jack! He's been getting up, moving around and walking more than ever. We've been to the playroom about 50 times. He loves the big window and the block table and the fact that they're all the way at the other end of the hall from us just means he has farther to walk and that's good!

They ran some tests on day 6 to check for chylothorax and he was negative. Yay! They also did an ultrasound of Jack's throat area to check for blood clots and he didn't have any. Another small victory! The drainage has just been really persistent and negative test results mean that the new blood flow is just causing Jack's body to have a harder time adjusting than most other kids do. Now we just wait for it to slow down.

On day 7 Jack got one tube out! Praise the Lord! The left side has been draining a lot less than the right side. The nurse practitioner came by yesterday morning and he told us that the plan is to take the one tube out and keep watching the other one. They've bumped him up on the diuretics to try to get rid of some of the fluid. He said that Dr. Dabal created a pathway between the two areas where the fluid sits so that if the fluid on the left does build back up it should be able to seep over to the right side and drain out of the remaining tube. Then once the right side dries up for the most part, they'll pull that tube. We'll continue on the diuretics for a while to make sure it doesn't build back up. We'll stay in the hospital for 2-3 days after the tube comes out to make sure it doesn't build back up quickly. Once we go home they'll monitor us on a weekly basis with chest x-rays and echoes to check for fluid. The hope is that it doesn't come back. However, it's likely that it will. He said that they like to get the kids home and to their own environment where they can move around more freely and eat better because those things will help with the fluid. But if Jack starts showing signs of being tired, breathing trouble, or eating trouble we need to bring him back immediately. He said to always pack a bag for the first couple of months when we come to the clinic because the likelihood that we will have to stay is high every time. He said if we do end up getting readmitted they usually will start with diuretics by IV to try to clear it back up and if that doesn't work there is always a possibility of having to get a tube back in to drain it. However, there is definitely a good possibility that we will go home and not have to be readmitted so we're believing and praying for that. And if we do have to be readmitted then we'll cross that bridge when we get there!

We've changed over to giving all meds by mouth which is not fun. It's usually 3-4 different things every 4 hours with a couple here and there in between. He screams and spits and cries. Not fun.

Having the second tube out is making a huge difference for him. He is happier and way more mobile. He takes off without us and we have to catch up before he pulls the last tube out! But happy and wild is good. Happy and wild is JACK!

POST-OP DAY 8

I can't believe it's already been over a week! We waited and dreaded this surgery for FOUR YEARS and now here we are, eight days post-op. It feels amazing to know it's behind us for good! And if we hadn't had to reschedule we would only be post-op day ONE right now so thank goodness for surprise schedule changes! We are about to head down to the arts and crafts party downstairs that Jack has been looking forward to all day! Our fingers are crossed that the third and final tube will come out in the next 2-3 days. That means home in less than a week!

SATURDAY, JUNE 18, 2016

24 Days Post-Op

"Grace and peace be yours in abundance through
the knowledge of God and of Jesus our Lord."

2 PETER 1:2

Well, here we are… Pushing a month in the hospital and I really can't believe we're in this boat again. I didn't foresee the Fontan recovery being this difficult. Yesterday a doctor that worked with us after Jack's Glenn came in and she looked at us with sad eyes and said, "Y'all just can't have an easy time, can you?" I guess not.

We made it home last Wednesday afternoon knowing that our chances of landing back in the CCU were pretty high, which was scary to me. I HATE the hospital life and being separated from H but I would rather know that Jack is completely well before we bring him home. But nevertheless, they let us go home with the promise that IF the fluid builds back up it will be over a longer period of time (days, not hours) and they will check him again on Friday. Friday morning we saw the cardiologist at the clinic and he said that the fluid was still there but that Jack was managing well and that it didn't seem to be building, just resting. He also looked at the growing infection around Jack's incision and started him on Keflex. We made an appointment to come back Monday at 11:00 to check everything again.

The weekend was WONDERFUL. Jack played and laughed and rolled in the floor with Harrison and it wasn't as scary to have him at home as I thought it would be. He was already two full weeks post-op and he felt great. He played outside with his friends and LOVED being home. Sunday night he went to bed feeling fine. No complaints. He woke up a few hours later crying that the infected area of his incision was hurting. I gave him some Motrin and he went back to sleep. Around 1:00am he woke up screaming and couldn't go back to sleep. I was really worried so I decided to just go ahead and take him in to the ER. I knew that we had an appointment in the clinic at 11 the next morning but I didn't want to wait if something more serious was going on. So me and Jack headed back to Children's. They did some blood work and after a few hours in the ER the doctor came in and told us we were being readmitted to treat the infection and before we knew it we were back in the CCU with all of our old friends (nurses).

Two days ago Jack had a little minor procedure where Dr. Dabal went in and cleaned out the infected area of Jack's incision. They took cultures so that he could tell exactly what kind of infection it is so that they can know for sure that they're treating it with the right antibiotics. Now Jack has a hole in his chest. I won't venture to guess the size but I'm pretty sure you could fit half of a golf ball down in there. They're packing it with gauze daily and bandaging it up and the goal is for it to close up from the bottom up, so that it will heal completely and not just close at the skin over the top of a hole. SO for now, big hole, big bandage. Uck.

Dr. Dabal told us the day we got re-admitted that even if Jack didn't have the infection we would have likely been readmitted anyway during our clinic visit because of that pesky fluid. So while Jack was getting IV antibiotics to treat the infection anyway they were just going to go ahead and get him back on some IV diuretics to hit that fluid hard too. They went ahead and told us on Wednesday that after two days of the maximum dose of IV diuretics Jack's fluid was being so persistent that they thought that he was going to need the pigtail tube to drain it. So they decided to go ahead and make plans to place the tube and clean out the incision at the same time on Thursday morning.

I went home to spend the night with H Wednesday night and came back early Thursday morning to be with Jack before the procedure. I brought Harrison with me because I knew seeing him would lift Jack's spirits before he had to go back for the procedure. As I was pulling into the parking deck my phone started ringing. It was Josh. He told me that he had good news. ALL of the fluid was gone. All of it.

That. Is. Not. Possible.

They had maxed Jack out on IV diuretics for DAYS and the fluid hadn't moved. They were 100% sure that it wasn't going to move at all. Not even a little. Hence the need for the tube. So for them to pull up an x-ray and say that it's GONE was unbelievable. The cardiologist told us that there was a big simultaneous gasp when the x-ray came up because everyone in the room was shocked.

That's just God. 100% y'all.

So they went ahead and planned for the procedure where they would clean out the infection but they didn't have to place the tube. Thank you Lord. We went down with Jack and talked to him until we had to leave so they could sedate him. I could hear him crying MOMMMMYYY until the door to the CI closed behind me. Ugh. Worst feeling ever. But they gave him the sedation drugs very quickly after that and he zoned out. He was awake the whole time but completely out of it. We got to go back and see him after and it probably only took 10 minutes. Dr.

Dabal said it went great and there wasn't really any infection in there. He said there were white blood cells which indicates that he was fighting an infection but no bacteria so that's good news. They sent cultures to make sure but he felt confident that nothing would grow there. He explained the hole and the packing and re-growing process.

Jack was so funny coming off of that sedation. At first it was kind of scary because his eyes were open but wouldn't fix on anything and when he would try to follow my voice and look at me his eyes would jump really fast like 100 times. I didn't like it. It passed pretty quickly though and then all of a sudden he looked over and said "I love you Mommy." Then he started talking silly. I said, "do you feel good?" He said, "Yea. YEA! YEAAAA!!!" Then he started asking for Harrison a THOUSAND times and screaming his name. His nurse just giggled at him. It wasn't long after that when he came back to his normal self and we got to head back up to our room in the CCU.

Since then we've just been hanging out. Jack has been on isolation until the cultures come back. So, he can't leave the room which is HORRIBLE for our little go-er and do-er. He's been driving us and his nurse friends crazy wanting out. But he's 100% his wild and silly self and ready to get back home again soon.

Today they took him off of all IV drugs and switched everything over to PO. They went ahead and got him a prescription for his antibiotic filled so we don't have to wait around on it forever when we get discharged tomorrow. (Oh! Did I forget to mention we are GOING HOME TOMORROW??) Once we're home, the plan will be the same as it was before. Frequent visits to the clinic for x-rays and echoes to check for fluid probably for a long time. But frequent visits to the clinic from HOME are better than daily x-rays at 5am in the hospital. So yay for going home tomorrow!! They taught Josh how to pack and dress his wound since, let's face it, Mommy cries at the very sight of it from a distance and Daddy is tough and brave. Josh will change it twice a day for a few days and then change to once a day. Dr. Dabal seems to think it will close up in a few days. I sure hope he's right about that. The sooner the better! As for the fluid, let's just pray we've seen the last of it!

I'm tired y'all. And this last week almost broke me. I came into the Fontan feeling so brave and so ready to put this chapter of our lives (the waiting for the Fontan chapter) behind us. I was scared but I was also confident that it would be different and we wouldn't have complications and setbacks. We had our fair share of complications after the Glenn and this time I felt sure would be easier. Boy was I wrong! Thankfully, the issues we've had this time around still don't compare to the recovery from the Glenn. Mostly because the complications we have experienced this time have been somewhat expected and completely manageable. After the Glenn, Jack was so sick the whole time and the doctors weren't sure how to fix him or even if they could. This time he has felt good for the most part and they have been able to get ahead of the problems the whole time so it hasn't felt as scary or overwhelming.

However, there are moments in this hospital life that my mind and my heart aren't on the same page. In my mind, I know that Jack is doing well and the infection and the fluid are manageable and treatable and simply setbacks that will keep us here longer but not dangerous or life-threatening. BUT in my heart, I've been terrified. Watching my baby go through all of this day in and day out, connected to machines, cut open, screaming in pain, writhing from withdrawals, needles poking him, people holding him down, on and on… It's just too much sometimes. It feels so unfair. When my friends all post pictures of their sweet kids playing at the park or swimming in the pool. I can't help but question why this has to be the life that was chosen for Jack. It's hard and it's scary and its unfair. And I want to scream or break things or do anything that will make all of this stop. But it doesn't stop. It can't. Because the reality is that this is the life we were given. Hand chosen for us by the Creator of the universe. And I don't know why. I don't know why my beautiful, happy, full-of-life little red-headed boy had to be the one to carry this burden. But I know that he carries it with a heck of a lot more grace than I do. And I'm sure he always will because this is the only version of life that he will ever know.

But as we walk through the hallways of this hospital filled with sick children and scared parents, life really comes into perspective. We will walk out of here soon. We will go home and eventually resume the life that we know. Jack will play in the yard and he will grow and we will have years of life and love and laughter with him ahead before we have to face the next step in this journey. Even though I would give anything to trade this life for a perfectly healthy one for Jack, I can be thankful for the good things. We are GOING HOME. Jack is RECOVERING. God is GOOD.

I watched a video this morning that reminded me that even before I was born God had called me to be the mother of a child with heart disease. Every moment of my life I was being prepared for this journey. Even in the toughest days of my life before Jack was born, when I was facing battles that felt so difficult and that I didn't understand, God was pruning me and preparing me for the even more difficult days ahead. And God's strength fills every single crevice of my weakness. He lifts me in those dark moments. He reminds me to turn my eyes to Him because He knows that He is the only place where my heart will find true peace. He calms my raging seas. Every single time. And let me tell you, my seas, they can REALLY RAGE. The hurt and the anger and the bitterness can all rear their ugly heads in my heart and I can go from zero to one hundred in one second flat for no specific reason and He's right there to talk me back down and remind me that everything is going to be okay. Every single time.

I am so thankful for God's grace. Though all of this God has continuously poured his grace over me and Josh and our family. We all struggled with the idea that the Fontan was coming. The idea of handing him over felt impossible. But we knew it had to be done. Jack couldn't live without it. So we prayed and waited. (And I cried. a lot.) And after four years or waiting and dreading and fearing that day, I can't believe that it was TWENTY-FOUR days ago! It's OVER. Done. In the past. There are moments when I seriously can't even wrap my brain around that. This has owned and defined our lives for years and now it's done. Thank you God.

The Fontan is not the end of our journey. It was a palliative, not curative procedure. It put a really GREAT band-aid on Jack's heart issue that will last a really long time. And for now we are thankful. We are looking forward to YEARS of peace and good health. As for the future, we are believing that it will be many years before we have to worry about the "next step."

PART 3

LIFE LESSONS

As I look back on all that we've been through, from hearing Jack's diagnosis to handing him over for surgery each time, from good news to bad news and everything in between, sometimes it doesn't even feel real. I look back and think, did that really happen to us? Is this really our life? Jack is now a thriving, healthy, wild, silly, funny, smart, handsome, growing little boy. Last summer he joined the swim team for the first time and he is currently in his third year of baseball. He continues to amaze us every single day with his resilience and strength. For Jack, this life is all he's ever known. He rarely ever mentions his scar or his surgeries. Cardiology appointments come once a year now and are usually very routine. They do an EKG and an echocardiogram. His cardiologist gives us an update on how his heart looks and sends us on our way for another year. At our last appointment I asked the dreaded question of what is next for us. He told us that at some point between the ages of eight and twelve they will begin to check the function of some of Jack's other organs. The

Fontan system that they created in Jack's body to allow blood to bypass his heart and go straight into his lungs helped relieve the pressure on his underdeveloped heart. However, it created more pressure for the other organs than they were intended to bear. So eventually, the next bump in the road that we will likely encounter will be issues with other organs before his heart begins to give us trouble. Some people live well into adulthood before needing further intervention. Others don't. As for Jack, only time will tell.

This journey with congenital heart disease has changed me forever. Before that day that we were told that Jack had CHD, I had never even heard of it. I look back on myself, the version of me that existed before that day, and I can see the way that God was molding and shaping my life to prepare me for this very life-altering moment. And all along, I had no idea. The experiences I was going through in the weeks, months and even years leading up to Jack's birth we're all shaping me into the person God wanted me to be so that I could take on this mountain that He knew was going to be placed in front of me. And yet on that day, I looked at that mountain and felt blind-sided. I tried so hard not to be angry with God. But I was. See, the way I looked at it, through my very human eyes, was that I was a good person, a Godly person even. I had just recently hit a rough patch in life that I felt somehow earned me the right to have it easy for a while. I felt like I had earned the right to some happy times. And suddenly bad things were happening and I felt like a victim. But I wasn't a victim. And Jack wasn't a victim. We were just people. Living life. And sometimes life is good and sometimes it's bad and most of the time it's just somewhere in between. And with all of that in mind, I want to tell you about some of the life lessons I have learned along the way.

LESSON 1:
Life is What We Make it and We Can Choose to Make it Good

"May the God of hope fill you with all joy and peace as you trust in Him, so that you may overflow with hope by the power of the Holy Spirit."

ROMANS 15:13

I can really get down sometimes. I can be the queen of the pity party when I want to be. I can wallow like no other. But never once in any of the times that I can remember when I spent time feeling sorry for myself or "letting myself be sad" (aka wallowing) do I remember those things bringing me any peace or joy.

Now friends, I'm not saying that we are always going to be filled with peace and joy. Life is not all butterflies and rainbows. Unfortunately, bad things do happen and sadness and sorrow are a part of life. But how we choose to spend our days is entirely up to us.

Choosing to find joy and search for peace in even the most difficult times is something that God has given us the power to do. Now, hear me say this. I don't know if this is something that can be mastered. I certainly haven't mastered it yet and I've been actively trying for several years. But trying helps. It gets you places. And peace comes. You just have to ask for it with a willing heart. You have to be willing and ready to accept it. And that is not always easy to do. It requires trusting God in ways that our human nature instinctively tells us not to do. But when we do make that choice, to give it to Him and trust that no matter the outcome He's got us, peace floods in and fills up all of the cracks inside of us that we can't fill ourselves.

What I mean by all of that is that life is really what you make it. You want to feel sorry for yourself all day long... Life will gladly remind you of all of the crappy things that have ever happened to you and you will start to build yourself a little mountain of past troubles that seem unfair. Suddenly you find yourself wallowing in sadness feeling angry at the world and jealous of everyone who doesn't have all of the same troubles as you.

But what if you actively choose to look at life from a different perspective? What if rather than counting your sorrows, you count your blessings instead? When I look at Jack and all of the bad things we've been through it would be easy for me to walk around, head hanging, feeling sorry for us. I could easily walk around complaining, and the truth is that most people would probably pat me on the back and tell me that I'm right and it really isn't fair and we don't deserve it. But who wants to live that way? Certainly not me. So instead, I choose to look at our situation with Jack with the mindset that things could have been worse. And things have been worse for many others. We are the lucky ones. And that is powerful and life changing. There is ALWAYS someone that has been through worse. And there is ALWAYS good to be found.

Please don't misunderstand. By no means do I want to downplay anything I have been through or anything you may have been through. Life sucks sometimes. Life can stop you in your tracks and rip everything that you thought was good right out of your hands. Life can be cruel. But no matter what bad, awful things happen to us... we have to wake up and do tomorrow. Life doesn't give us a choice. So, my friend, when the bad comes, grieve it. Wallow in it for however long you need to. Get angry and throw things and yell and scream and do whatever you need to do. I've done it. Sometimes those things are just a part of the process. But when you're done, get up and begin that search for peace. Don't let the darkness swallow you up. Your life has a meaning and a purpose and all of the bad can be meaningful if you allow it to be. But you can't let it overcome you. You have to choose joy for yourself. You have to let go of the guilt and know that whatever bad has happened, you deserve joy and happiness and laughter and ultimately, peace.

And remember, God doesn't allow anything to happen to anyone that He can't use. I didn't ask to be used. In fact, I told you before that if God Himself had knocked on my door and offered me the greatest platform in the world in exchange for the health of my firstborn son, it would have been a hard no from me. But He didn't ask. And I'm here. And that's okay. Because I truly and completely believe that our story matters. I believe that Jack's life matters. And I'm not going to waste it sitting around feeling sorry for us or putting limits on what God can do. Instead, I choose joy. I choose laughter. I choose faith. I choose to be used by the Creator who made Jack exactly the way he is through this story that He chose for us long before any of us ever took a breath.

"And after you have suffered a little while, the God of all grace [who imparts all blessing and favor], Who has called you to His [own] eternal glory in Christ Jesus, will Himself complete and make you what you ought to be, establish and ground you securely, and strengthen, and settle you."

1 PETER 5:10

LESSON 2:

God is Good, Even When Life is Bad

"The Lord is good to all, and His tender
mercies are over all His works."

PSALM 145:9

So this one starts with Eve. Remember her? First girl God ever made. Yea... She basically messed us all up. Thanks a lot sister. Totally kidding. Well, sort of. But really, it actually does start with her. Because Eve made a choice that day in the garden that had a ripple effect that is still messing up our lives today.

Enter sin.

So I'm sure you're wondering what Eve's crappy choice has to do with me and you but the answer is EVERYTHING. Eve brought sin into the world. And sin is the cause for all of the bad things that happen in the world, even today. See, when Eve sinned, death became a reality. Before Eve took a bite out of that fruit, everything was perfect. Adam and Eve were in the presence of God in absolute and total perfection. But God allowed them free will. He wanted them to love and serve Him out of the desire of their hearts, not because He forced them to. And unfortunately, the enemy was there that day speaking lies into their spirits, much like he does to you and me today. And Eve bought in, much like we often do.

The way I look at it, it didn't have to be Eve. Sure, she made a mistake. But sometimes I think she gets a bad rap. Because if it had been me in her place, would I not have made the same choice she made? Do I not question God and believe the lies of the enemy all the time. Sure I do. So do you. It's called human nature. We are weak. We are selfish. We are fallen. But God didn't just leave Adam and Eve there to rot. He could have. Actually, He could have just wiped them completely off the planet and started over. But He didn't. God loved them enough to help them clean up their own mess. Sure, there were earthly consequences like work, labor and death. But there were also provisions. He gave them clothing and food and a way to atone for their mistakes. Because y'all, even though life can be bad, God is still good. All the time. No matter what.

When I sat in my hospital bed that first night feeling helpless, I cried out to God. "WHY is this happening? Why would you allow this? I just don't understand. I've been through so much. This baby was supposed to be my joy. It doesn't make sense." That day, I questioned God just like Eve did in the garden. My finite human mind couldn't possibly fathom how this bad, horrible, awful thing could ever be good. Jack was a perfect, innocent baby. Incapable of doing anything wrong and yet his body was broken. Years of my life that I had spent dreaming of becoming a mother led me to this day. It was supposed to be the happiest day of my life. And suddenly, nothing made sense. My faith was shaken.

One of the hardest lessons I've learned along this journey is to accept that this bad thing that happened to me was not something God created and set before me. It was something that was created as a result of the sin that you and I commit daily. Sin brought forth death and from that seed all destruction and darkness was born into the world. That wasn't God's choice. It was ours.

Deep, I know.

But friends, here is the good news. Not only did God send his only son to die on the cross to save us from the eternal damnation that awaits us as a result of our sin, but He didn't stop there. He could have just said, alright. I did the hard thing. Jesus came and suffered and died and the veil was torn and sin and death were defeated and now all who choose to call me Father will have freedom from their sin and an eternity with me in heaven. But He loves us enough to love us even while we are still sinners. Y'all. This is BIG.

God doesn't cause bad things to happen to us. But because of sin they do happen. And when they do, He chooses to pour grace, mercy and love into us so that we can walk through the trials and hardships that this world brings. Not only do we get eternal salvation but we get love and mercy in the moment. That is a good God, friends.

I understand. For the unbeliever or the fence-sitter, this is hard to fathom. You're asking so many questions right now. Maybe it even makes you mad. Because you feel like things have happened to you and you didn't feel God's love and mercy and grace. You felt alone. You felt scared. And you don't feel like anyone rode in to rescue you. I get it. I've been there. But all of these spiritual battles we are facing are inside of us. We too often listen to the enemy who is constantly whispering in our ears, just like he did to Eve that day, telling us that God is not who He says He is. That He doesn't really love us and if He did then He wouldn't let these bad things happen to us. But ALL of those things are LIES. And when you choose to believe them, you are allowing the enemy to have victory over your life. That is not what God wants for you. God wants you to live in peace. He wants you to gain the full understanding of who He is and how great His love is for you. But you can't get there until you let go

of those lies you are holding onto. Bitterness, doubt and anger…
it only hurts you. And that is exactly what the enemy wants.

See, through all of the bad times, on the darkest of days
when I felt completely alone and abandoned by God, I look
back and I can see Him etching a path for me. His plan was, and
still is beyond my understanding. In my time on this earth I will
never know why God chose Jack. And it will always hurt. And
I will always resent it and wish with every single breath that I
take that I could change it. But He allowed this for a reason.
God looks at us through eternal lenses. He sees more than just
this fleeting moment we are in. He sees our forever. And much
like us allowing our children to fall down while they are learning to walk, He allows us to be molded through trials because
ultimately, this life is only a moment and our eternity is what
matters the most. God loves me enough to let me fall. But He
never leaves me or forsakes me. Even when I can't feel Him.
Even when I don't understand. God is good and His plan for me
is what is best for me.

"When you pass through the waters, I will be with you, and through the
rivers, they will not overwhelm you. When you walk through the fire, you
will not be burned or scorched, nor will the flame kindle upon you."

ISAIAH 43:2

LESSON 3:
Being Different is a Good Thing

"I knew you before I formed you in your mother's womb. Before you were born I set you apart and appointed you as my prophet to the nations."

JEREMIAH 1:5

I used to struggle with the idea that Jack would be different. Not because it bothered me. I have thought he was perfect since the first time I laid eyes on him and to be honest, I just think his scar makes him even cuter. But I worried about how his scar and his physical limitations would affect him in the long run. We've always known that Jack wouldn't be able to do some things that require a lot of physical stamina like contact sports, for example. It just scared me that he would struggle with being different. I never wanted him to have to struggle any more than he already has. But I work in a high school and I know firsthand that kids can be mean. I guess, the way I looked at it, Jack had already been through enough. It didn't seem fair that after all he's been through already, that he now has to live the rest of his life being different from all of the other kids.

But one day it just occurred to me that as Jack's parents, Josh and I get to play a role in how he views himself. So we began to remind him often of how powerful that scar on his chest is. His "zipper" is his badge of war. His daily reminder that if he can conquer all that he has already conquered, there isn't anything he can't do.

And little by little, God has been shaping him into the person that he is going to become. And guess what? So far, Jack has never once been bothered by his scar or the fact that he is different. After all of that worrying I did over the years, he has grown into a kid who it hasn't affected at all. And for the things we thought he would never be able to do, God has provided a way. Swim, for example. Jack fell in love with swimming a few years ago. And he's really good at it. So we cautiously asked our cardiologist about it. And he said what he always says... Jack gets to set his own limits. If Jack can swim... more power to him. And so he does. Sometimes he stops in the middle of the lane and grabs the rope to rest. And that's okay. As the years go by, he learns more and more about his own limitations. And they're always smaller than we could have imagined. Sometimes at swim practice I just sit there and let the tears fall. I can't believe that he is here now, swimming, laughing, living. He might not be the fastest swimmer on the team but he's out there doing his thing and living his life. And what a blessing it is for me to get to watch.

Jack defines his own normal. Is he the same as everyone else? No. But what is "normal" anyway? Jack likes video games. Something I always swore I would never let my kids do... you know back before I became a parent when I thought I knew everything there was to know about how to raise perfect kids. Jack loves swimming and baseball. Two things I was sure he would never be able to do. Jack likes school. He loves to read. He doesn't always like doing his homework but loves being praised when he does it well. He is the pickiest eater on the planet. He is incredibly loving. He loves to help people. He doesn't mind trying new things and meeting new people. He is an extraordinary kid. And he's unique. There are no other kids just like Jack. And

I can't imagine him being any other way.

As a parent you basically have two choices: you can accept your kids the way they are and love the things they love, or you can try to force them to be who you want them to be and to love the things you want them to love. This choice isn't always black and white. Sometimes the things your kids love don't seem like what's best for them. You feel like as the parent you have to steer your kids in the right direction. And that's totally acceptable and the right thing to do... But in some cases, you just don't get what you thought you wanted and you have to choose to love and embrace your kids for exactly who they are.

One of the most valuable lessons I have learned on this journey is to embrace the moment I am in with the kid that God gave me exactly the way that he is. I get to watch Jack jump into the pool with true joy in his spirit. I let him kick my butt at Mario-Kart on a regular basis because he thinks beating me is hilarious and his laugh is pretty much my favorite sound. I wipe his tears off his face as he cries about not wanting to go to school on rainy days because he's scared of storms. And I do my best to teach him Jesus and remind him that God made him unique and special and extraordinary and that he is exceptionally loved exactly the way he is.

I've learned over the past few years what I believe the truly important things are when it comes to parenting. Before I became a mom, I daydreamed about things like baseball games and big family vacations. But in reality, parenting is about the little moments. It's about the conversations we have on the way to school in the morning. It's about the bedtime stories and prayers we say at night. It's about decorating the Christmas tree, dancing in the kitchen and singing at the top of our lungs. It's about setting the example and being there for them every single time they need us. Ultimately, parenting is about leading our kids to

Christ and raising them to be kind, self-sufficient human beings.

Being a mother has taught me so many valuable lessons about life. One of those lessons is that there are no do-overs. And the sooner we choose to love and accept our kids the exact way they are, the sooner we teach our children to love and embrace their differences rather than always looking at themselves through the lens of comparison, the sooner we get to watch our children blossom into the unique and perfect little people that God created them to be. So friends, let's empower our children to love themselves, flaws, scars, differences and all.

LESSON 4:

Just Say No to Fear

"Fear not, for I am with you; be not dismayed, for I
am your God; I will strengthen you, I will help you,
I will uphold you with my righteous right hand."

ISAIAH 41:10

I've never really been a fan of scary movies. I just don't really get the concept of paying money to sit in a theater and feel terrified. I've pretty much always been a chicken when it comes to those kinds of things. When I was a teenager and my friends and I would go to judgment houses, I wouldn't go into Hell. I mean, realistically, I felt pretty certain that I wasn't headed there anyway so why go in and get myself all worked up over it.

You see friends, I'm the kind of person who emotionally connects too much. I can't help it. It's just part of who I am. I cry at all movies. Happy or sad. I cry reading books. I cry listening to music. I literally cannot make it through any kind of performance that my children do at church or at their school without making a total and complete fool of myself and shaming my husband beyond words. Hallmark Christmas movies, with all of those super sappy, totally predictable happily ever after endings... forget it. Tears for days. I'm just so happy for that fictional hard working business woman who found her prince charming in the cereal aisle at the grocery store.

I think this instinct inside of me that causes me to blubber like a baby in front of my classroom full of students every single time that Doodle dies in "The Scarlet Ibis" is also the same one that causes me to be so afraid of being afraid. I don't just get scared of something or get upset by something and then just forget about it later. I lose sleep over Doodle every semester y'all. Things stay with me. And that is exactly how fear works. It grabs onto us and then slowly begins to rip us apart.

Josh took me to see a new movie a few weeks ago. I begged him to let us see something funny but he was determined that we had to see "First Man." (If you're not familiar, this is the movie where Ryan Gosling plays the role of Neil Armstrong.) Not even ten minutes into the movie, their little toddler daughter passes away. Y'all. I had to get up and leave the theater. I called my sis-ter from the bathroom stall having a full-on panic attack. Not like, I got upset and cried a few tears. No. Like I hyperventilated in the bathroom and had to go to the car to get my inhaler so that I could breathe again.

Since Jack was born, I don't do movies or TV shows about kids who are sick, in danger, etc. It's too much and I know my own limitations. This one caught me by surprise. I didn't know anything about Neil Armstrong's family. So watching them lower their daughter's tiny casket into the ground was too much for me. It was too much because it was dancing all over my worst and most intimate fear. This is one I do not talk about. Ever. But I'm feeling extra vulnerable today so I'm going to share it with you.

Six years ago my life stopped dead in its tracks. My whole world became completely and totally engulfed in congenital heart disease. It changed every aspect of my life. It completely and forever changed the way that I view the world. My life is no longer about me. It is about the two little people that God allowed me to bring into this world. And my greatest, deepest and most intense fear is that I could lose one of them.

When you first hear that your child is being diagnosed with a life threatening illness, you immediately take to Google to find out everything you can about that illness. Or, at least that is what I did. And Google, while most of the time is extremely helpful, sometimes is harmful too. You've heard that joke where someone has a runny nose, checks their symptoms in Google and diagnoses themselves with stage 4 cancer? Yea, it's kind of like that. But more real. And much more terrifying.

Immediately when Jack was born I started researching his particular CHD. I dove head first into the rabbit hole and didn't come back out for days. I read and printed and studied everything I could find. Which was helpful for the most part because it helped me understand his anatomy and what the doctors' plan was for him. But along with helpful understanding, I also gained gripping fear. See, for every scientifically helpful article I found about CHD, there were 10 articles about kids born with CHD. And while some of those stories were positive and uplifting, it only takes a few bad ones to take down the heart of a scared momma. I would scroll through pictures of these precious babies who fought their battles with CHD until they couldn't fight anymore. And every single time I would wonder... what if this is us? What if this is God's plan for Jack. And my heart would tremble with fear that no amount of funny movies or happy thoughts could conquer.

One day I came across the story of a precious little guy named Liam. Liam's story just grabbed my heart. I knew I should avoid it. But I couldn't. So I started following him. When Liam would get sick I would ask for prayer for him at church. I would wait anxiously for days to hear updates on him. And then one day, the update came. Liam lost his battle with CHD. And on that day, a piece of my heart broke forever. I didn't know Liam. I didn't know his family. But I felt connected to them because they had walked down this path that my family was on. And when Liam died, I didn't know how to process it. I struggled with immense levels of unrealistic fears and intense worry. I couldn't sleep. I would lie awake at night and cry in my bed and just beg God not to take Jack. It completely broke me.

Fear has a way of taking root inside of us and burning us up from the inside out. When we allow one "what if" thought into our brain, they begin to spread like wildfire. And fear is one of the enemy's favorite tools to use against us. The Bible says that he comes to steal, kill and destroy. And fear can be used as the tool to do all of those things. Fear can steal our joy and security. It can rob us of the moment we are in for fear of what could happen tomorrow. Fear can kill our peace and destroy our lives entirely.

I had allowed fear to take over and I was living in a state of terror that I couldn't seem to overcome. My mind was constantly consumed with the darkest thoughts of a million different horrible scenarios that could possibly play out in our lives. I became intensely paranoid and began feeling like I needed constant reassurance from Jack's medical team which I obtained through a series of polite emails the sheer volume of which some might consider brazen harassment. (One of those moments, undoubtedly, when Jack's cardiologist questioned all of his life decisions.) I became someone I didn't recognize. And I told myself it was all in the name of love. The love I had for Jack was causing me to be irrational. I allowed myself to believe that it was natural to feel the way I felt, given our circumstances. But, friends, I was SO wrong.

Eventually, through a time of deep and meaningful soul searching and spiritual growth, I learned that fear has no power that we do not give to it. Let me say that again for our friends in the back… fear has no power that we do not give to it.

Allow me to explain. As I started spending more and more time in the Bible, I started to see a pattern. All of the scripture that I was drawn to had to do with fear. And there was a lot of it!

"Fear not, for I am with you; be not dismayed, for I am your God;
I will strengthen you, I will help you, I will uphold you with my righteous
right hand."

ISAIAH 41:10

"Do not be anxious about anything, but in everything by prayer and sup-
plication with thanksgiving let your requests be made known to God."

PHILIPPIANS 4:6

"For you did not receive the spirit of slavery to fall back into fear,
but you have received the Spirit of adoption as sons, by whom we cry,
'Abba! Father!'"

ROMANS 8:15

"There is no fear in love, but perfect love casts out fear. For fear has to
do with punishment, and whoever fears has not been perfected in love.
We love because he first loved us."

1 JOHN 4:18-19

"Even though I walk through the valley of the shadow of death, I will fear
no evil, for you are with me; your rod and your staff, they comfort me."

PSALM 23:4

I could keep going all day long. The bottom line is that God does not want us to fear. And realistically, no amount of worry-ing, crying or, let's be real, trying to prepare myself for the worst, could ever add a single day to my children's lives. It's never going to be up to me. So I have to find a way to accept that I'm not the one in control.

And that is the breakthrough moment y'all. I hope you're listening. This is good stuff right here.

I'm not in control. I have zero control.

My. Children. Are. Not. Mine.

Yes, I carried them in my womb and yes I love them with every single ounce of my being but they don't actually belong to me. They belong to their Creator. And He is the one who is in control. He is the one who breathed life into them. He is the one that designed them to be the perfect, wild, messy, silly little creatures that they are. He held them in His hands long before I ever laid eyes on them. He carved out a path for them and He sent his only son to die on a cross for them and no matter what may come during this brief and fleeting lifetime we are in He has a place for them in eternity with Him. Yall. Can I get an AMEN?

No amount of loving my children, caring for them, rocking them to sleep, buying them all the Christmas presents they could ever want, teaching them life lessons, or anything else I could ever do within my human power as a mother could ever come close to what God can do, will do and has done for them. And that is more than enough reassurance for me.

Resting in the assurance that God is in control is the only method I have ever found that truly allows me to let go of my fears. Now, don't get me wrong. I go and pick them back up all the time. I'm human. I'm a mom. And I love deeply. So fear is unfortunately natural. I do, however, now know how to combat those fears when they start to rise up inside of me. I hit my knees. And God's grace is sufficient every single time.

LESSON 5:

Life Goes On

"Time is very slow for those who wait. Very fast for those who are scared. Very long for those who lament. Very short for those who celebrate. But for those who love, time is eternal."

WILLIAM SHAKESPEARE

Well friends, we've made it. The last chapter. One more life lesson that I want to share with you before our time together is over. This last one is for all of us. Life goes on.

I find myself lately wishing I could stop the clock. The days, weeks and years are beginning to fly by. But I believe that is a sign that we are in a period of celebration in life right now. And so I won't complain. What are we celebrating, you ask? Everything. We are celebrating everything.

It took me a long time to find the balance of this new "normal" that we found ourselves in. Once Jack's surgeries were over I would find myself occasionally relaxing and I would suddenly panic and think-- my guard isn't up... what am I doing?? - But then I hear this still small voice that tells me to stop and look around. And when I do, I hear laughter. I see piles of student essays I need to grade and the laundry is piled to the ceiling and someone needs a cup of milk and someone needs cupcakes for their class and I forgot to make their haircut appointments before their school pictures and the list goes on and on. But above all of that noise, I hear laughter.

Seven years ago we watched our son code and go limp and lifeless on a tiny little hospital bed. The world in that moment was frozen. The days dragged on for what felt like years. Answers were few and far between. Fear dripped from the ceiling tiles and hung in a dark cloud above us, stealing away any sense of peace that we might have been able to muster. In those days I felt like I had been robbed of the future I had spent my entire life planning and praying for. I didn't understand the world anymore. What had always been simple, black and white suddenly beamed so many different colors. And in every different color there were questions and chaos that my mind couldn't navigate. The earth as I knew it had shifted on its axis, never to go back again.

In those days I couldn't have imagined the life we have now. No, it's not perfect. Jack's CHD didn't magically go away. And all of my fears for his life and his future didn't somehow diminish when the last set of discharge papers were handed to us. But something else happened. Life went on. Somewhat unexpectedly, I think.

I guess when you get so wrapped up in what is happening inside a very specific moment of your life, you forget that time doesn't stop for you. I mean, I really always believed that we would get past the Fontan and that Jack would be okay and that we would have a life post-Fontan that didn't revolve around "the next open heart surgery." But sometimes when I listen to Jack reading me a story or when I watch him run around chasing his brother through the house or when I watch him jump into the pool, fearless and full of life, I just can't even believe that we're here. That time passed and we made it to the other side. He's growing. He's strong and healthy and wild and hilarious and precious and wonderful and amazing. And he's here. And, no. I don't know what tomorrow holds. But I know that I don't want to spend my life waiting for the next shoe to drop. I want to live for today. I want to laugh with my kids and listen to their daddy pray for them and watch them grow and thank God every single chance I get for giving us today. And I choose to put my trust in Him for tomorrow.

"For I know the plans I have for you," declares the Lord. "Plans to prosper you and not harm you. Plans to give you hope and a future."

JEREMIAH 29:11

ACKNOWLEDGMENTS

TO MY FAMILY AND FRIENDS:

I grew up with the privilege of knowing the second greatest person to ever walk the face of the planet. We called her Maw-Maw and I am eternally grateful that God saw fit to let me spend my first 17 years with her. For the rest of my days, I doubt I will ever see anyone live more like Jesus than she did and I am overwhelmed with gratitude for the example that she set for me. So much of who I am is evident on the pages of this book and so much of who I am is credited to her.

On days in my life when I felt inadequate, I could always count on my sister to remind me of who I am and what God put me on this earth to do. She is my ultimate cheerleader and my very best friend. She knows who I am way down in my soul and she fully accepts and loves me with no limitations.

About a year ago she called me to tell me that she had directed a friend of hers to my blog. He was going through a difficult time in his life and she pointed him in the direction of words that she truly believed in. She had been encouraging me to compile my blog posts into a book for years but on this day it stuck. I sat down that evening and began working on it. So in large part, the credit for this little adventure goes to her. If she had not spent her life believing in me, supporting me and encouraging me, I don't know who I would be.

From day one of this book journey Josh has been behind me 100%. He let me slip away to a peaceful, quiet room while he entertained our wild boys on a regular basis so I could write. He has done ALL of the legwork to turn my words into an actual book. He has poured countless hours into making this little dream of mine a reality. And he did all of it because he truly believes in me and in our story. I can't say enough about the Godly husband and father he has grown into over our decade-and-a-half that we have spent together so far and I am undeniably grateful that God chose us for each other and that we get to do this life together.

My mom was the first person to read my full manuscript. True to form, she read the whole thing in a few short hours and then called me gushing about the complete state of awe she was in at the person she brought into the world. My dad, also true to form, was the first person to tell me not to take the first publishing deal I was offered. My mom and dad think I hung the moon. Always have. Always will. They are my biggest fans and they've spent my entire life loving me and my three sisters, providing for us and celebrating each and every victory. I could never thank them enough for all that they've done for me but I hope they can see the evidence of a daughter well raised on the pages of this book.

To my Aunt Tina, thank you for your bottomless well of wisdom from which I am constantly seeking to dip my cup.

To my amazing mother-in-law, Wendy, thank you for sharing your son with me long before you were ready to let him go and thank you for loving me like one of your own since the day we met.

To my friends and co-workers who have stood beside me, been a shoulder to cry on and cheered me on throughout the course of this journey, thank you. Your friendship means more to me than I could ever express.

To our church families both at Mount Vernon Baptist Church and Glory Fellowship Baptist Church, thank you for all of the love and support you have shown our family over the years.

There are so many other family members and close friends who I want to thank. If I said everything I am feeling on the inside it would take up another whole book. So instead I will say this, to all of the people who have loved me, supported me, prayed for me and encouraged me over the years, thank you.

TO ALL OF THE MEDICAL PROFESSIONALS WE'VE COME TO KNOW AND LOVE:

Dr. Law, where do I begin? Thank you first and foremost for dedicating your life's work to kids like Jack. It has been evident to me for many years now that CHD is not just your job, it's something you feel passionate about. We are eternally grateful to you for the good work you do on behalf of all of us who cannot do it ourselves. Thank you for always being honest with me. Thank you for always giving me as much time as I need, even though your job is demanding and you are undoubtedly needed in other places. Thank you for answering every single one of my crazy, emotional emails. Once, in response to one of those emotionally driven, scared-momma emails, you told me that you truly believed that Jack will grow up, go to college and have a life beyond CHD. In those few simple words, you saved me. Thank you.

Thank you to the man whose hands have mended our son's small heart on more than one occasion. Thank you to the surgeon who stood in our prayer circle and prayed with us over our sick baby. Thank you to the incredibly busy doctor who carved time into his daily routine to come check on us and provide us with some much-needed reassurance. Dr. Dabal, you have always gone far beyond the call of duty and I am convinced that God doesn't make them any better than you. Thank you for your dedication to, not just your work, but our son's life.

Dr. Alten came bee bopping in the night that I was holding a towel to my son's mouth as he spewed blood all over his hospital bed. He saw my tears and said, "why are you crying, it's just blood." While in that moment, I'm not going to lie, a small part of me wanted to punch this stranger right in the face, he quickly became one of my favorite people I'd ever met. Dr. Alten flew in like a superhero and saved the day for us. His light-hearted nature lifted some of the darkness from our little corner of the world and his God-given knack for doing his job well saved our son's life. For the decisions he made and the work that he did to turn our situation around and give our son a second chance, I am eternally grateful.

I wish I could list out all of the other medical professionals who impacted our journey but that would take days and I could not possibly do that list justice. So, instead, I will give a heartfelt thank you to every doctor, nurse and medical professional who we met along the way. The work that you all do is unimaginably difficult on so many levels. Thank you for doing it wholeheartedly and loving and caring for your patients fully every single day. You are world-changers and I consider us exceptionally blessed to have gotten to cross paths with each and every one of you.

TO JACK AND HARRISON:

It is my greatest prayer that you will both follow Jesus all of the days of your life. It is the greatest honor of my life to be your mom and to get to help you grow into who you're going to become. You are fiercely loved.

Made in the USA
Columbia, SC
04 January 2020

86141677R00124